ANITISMO

TABLE OF CONTENTS

CHAPTER 1

LOST CIVILIZATION OF
THE PHILIPPINES

The ancient chronicles of Jesuit and Hispanic friars say that upon the arrival of the first Spaniards, the coasts of the Visayas and even in Manila, there were many converts to Mohammedanism, and even more could be found in Mindanao that were converted by the islamic teachers from Borneo. So, if we are to find the true Philippine religion at its purest, we must look to the mountainous regions of the North. Knowing how to distinguish the True Religion from those that were influenced by the Hindu, Mohammedan and Christian grafts can be difficult, but the true Philippine religion is still intact, not only among the Itnegs (Tinguians), but in the legends, advice and superstitions of the Tagalog's, Visayan's, Bicolano's, Kapampangan's, Zambaleno's, Pangasinero's and other Filipino ethnic groups.

It is known that in the beginning the true religion of the Philippines was the same from the most southern point of Mindanao to the extreme north of Luzon. This religion was Anitism or the Cult of the Anito which means souls of the ancient ones or ancestors, and we have discovered also that Anitism has a vast and diverse Pantheon involving gods, animals, mountains, rivers, stars, supernatural beings and other elements.

It also has its own modern spiritism and was probably the origin of the cult of the Romanist Saints. In the overseas Museums and Libraries such as the National Library of Madrid, the Philippine library of the General Tobacco Company from Barcelona, the archives of the University of Sto.Tomas, and Convent of San Agustin in Manila, we have found the first editions of the oldest chronicles about the Philippines. We can follow these step by step from the first news that the Jesuit Pedro Quirino gave from 1604 Which were reproduced successively by the Jesuit Colin (year 1663), the Augustinian Gaspar from San Agustin and the Franciscan Francisco from San Antonio. We also saw the works of Fr. Plascencia, Grijalva, Morga, González de Mendoza, Aduarte and other Dominicans and friars.

Morga says that from Camarines to near Manila and from Manila to Cagayan, were Filipinos that practiced Anitism, some traditions say: it is known that Manila and its regions, were not natives of the island, but came to it in ancient times, that they were from the Malayan islands and from other remote islands and provinces. He adds that a few years before the Spaniards arrived, Mohammedans from Borneo that were Islamic teachers had come to preach their sect by distributing booklets and that those from Manila were already interacting with the Moors. Grijalva in his Chronicle of the order of San Augustine 1624 writes: In Manila and in Tondo, many people were affected by the sect because of the trade they had in Borneo, the ones arriving in Luzon married in the islands and integrated into society, they taught, gave lessons, and performed ceremonies. So, many of the islands began to adopt the traditions of the Moors even adopting Moorish names; they're teachings and beliefs spread so fast throughout the Philippines that the arrival of the Spaniards was delayed by the hands of Datu Lapu Lapu, because at the time the conquistadors arrived in the Philippines all the other religions, opinions, and beliefs were already heard by the Filipinos.

The Moors and other islanders who were not under the

control of the government in the Philippines, had been influenced by other religious teachers who came to them to preach from the Straits of Malacca and the Red Sea. One account from the conquest of Luzon dated on April, 20, 1572, which is preserved in the Archives of India, and which Mr. Wenceslao Retana reproduces in his Archive says: "In these towns closest to the sea they do not eat any pork, which the Moors taught them. but if you ask them, they say they do not know Muhammad or his law."

The truth is that some who have been to Borneo understand some things and can read some words from the Koran; however, they are very few. Traditionally, Filipinos give reverence and worship to the elements such as sun and the moon; this is commonly found in all the islands to some degree. This is what I have seen so far since we have been researching here, they have beliefs in the elements, animals, stars and other things such as the ancestors that they adore. From what is transcribed, it is clearly evidenced that the Filipino Religion in Manila and nearby, was mixed with Anitism, Buddhism, Brahmanism and Mohammedanism brought by the Malays of Borneo, and it is further evidenced by the Sanskrit and Malay terms mixed in the vocabulary of their theogony, such as Bathala or Badhala (Lord) but these terms are not used in the mountains and Northern provinces. Until now in Maguindanao they have Hindu gods that they call Mahesvara (Mahaswara or Shiva), Kala (goddess of death), Sri (Siri), Berma (Birma or Brahma) and Bisnu (Wishnú).

In the Philippines, then, before Mohammedanism and Hinduism the true religion of the Philippines could be found to be more pure every time we moved northward away from the South, where Malaysian, Hindu and Mohammedan immigrants came from. So, in the immediate vicinity of the Itnegs and other mountain tribes, we believe that is where the true Filipino religion is most conserved and pure. The Philippine religion is still prominent in Ilocos, Cagayan,

Isabela and other provinces of northern Luzon, it is here that the legends of the first religion of the Philippines is preserved, and this knowledge will serve best in order to untangle the many errors of the early Spanish chroniclers.

Hindus, especially Buddhists, made many converts throughout Java and throughout Malaysia which only in 1478 fell to the Mohammedans, that is 60 years before the Dutch invasion. According to the Javanese legends, the Hindus came to that island 78 years before Christ and according to the records of Malacca, the first Malays came out of the territory of the Minangkabau River (which is in the interior of Sumatra between the Djambi and Palembang rivers) and Lueron to found the cities of Malacca, Djohor and Singapore, in the twelfth century.

The German Doctor Semper says that there were various Malaysian emigrations in the 13th, 14th, and 15th centuries, probably in one of those emigrations they reached the Philippines; but wouldn't it also be possible that the Filipinos were the ones who populated the islands of Malaysia? and that emigrations started on the contrary, from our Archipelago pushed by the strong winds coming down from the North? This I asked in 1886. The truth is that when the first Spaniards went to Borneo, they found the Son of Lakandula, the King of Manila.

I was Speaking one day of these supposed Malaysian emigrations with the emperor's studious master of ceremonies from Japan, Mr. Fujita, he confirmed that the emigrations must have come from the North, and not from the South, and that Filipinos may be related to the Japanese. Remember that in Oceania there are the remnants of a lost great civilization, according to the great Geographer and Historian Reclusin in the Mariana Islands they have discovered very interesting ruins that the "know it all" Spaniards we had around here twenty years ago, did not know about. There is even A gigantic prehistoric statue from Oceania preserved in the British Museum and we are sure that if excavations are made in the caves, secret tombs, forgotten temples, and underground vaults, that hidden megaliths, precious artifacts, and other remnants of this great lost civilization can be found in The Philippines. I myself have seen some of these ancient statues and artifacts In the Bulacan caves (banks of the Pasig), Pangibalon hill, (Visayas), Madías de Iloilo, and in Nasso (Panay).

CHAPTER 2

THE FIRST TESTAMENT

The first testaments about this religion Anitismo, we find in the accounts of Lombard Antonio Pigáfetta, Magellan's chronicler. Pigafetta began chronicling all that was encountered and discovered in our archipelago, by the Spaniards beginning in 1521. Pigafetta tells that the natives of Limasawa, an island between Surigao and Butuan, called Their god Abba , which he described as a frightening deity made of wood and was hollow at the back, this was in Cebu, It's legs and arms were spread, feet raised, a very wide face and an open mouth revealing four long fangs like those of a wild boar; On the shores of that island there were many temples ... where food was offered to the deities or souls of the ancestors; but in cases of a more serious nature, they slaughtered a pig. Pigafetta called the ceremony the 'consecration of the pig'.

They also feared a large black bird, which, according to them, perched at night on the roof of their houses and cawed, that made the dogs howl and scratch until dawn. This entity was probably the fabulous Bauwa that according to the Visayans, is an Aswang which metamorphosed in prehistoric times, this bird was purely sacred like the Kumaw of the Ilocano; but Quirino interpreted it as the raven and even added that it was considered to be as the protector of the land; but he couldn't recollect if the raven had been worshiped by the Filipinos.

According to a report from Governor Legaspi sent to the

King of Spain in 1570, even before reaching Manila. The Visayas had no Idols or temples (which was incorrect), except for a small temple they called Olango, The name of their god was Diuata and its priestesses, the babaylans, who performed sacrifices and ceremonies (maganitos) and noted that they had golden hair, according to other accounts they held a gold medallion with the statue of the Anito and a reed in their other hand. The following account of the ceremony witnessed is given:

" The ceremony begins, he says with the babaylan dancing, and incorporates with adoration many scary eff ects and visages, looking up to the sky every now and then, manifesting visions and conversing with spirits, then the Babaylan goes back to dance until such a point that there is an effect as if this earth is falling and the sky dims with a diabolical color, And it's like this for a long time until the babaylan comes back to some normal state and It relays a thousand tales that the Gods has told it. The people offer up great sacrifices because the result they desired was achieved. If the sacrifice is an animal the spear is thrust into it and the priestess begins to dance and the people collect the blood to bring it to the sick, and the meat is distributed among all but as a traditional offering the priestess is given the best part of the pig in addition to the offerings given for her services".

Regarding the aforementioned account in another report from the year 1572 says in turn: "offerings and sacrifices in what I have seen, each of them has many Idols at home in which they worship. They call one God Bátala, he is an idol but the main one they have is called Ansí, and another name is Diobata (diuata) at least among the painted tribes, they call him Ansi; the natives on the island of Luzon commonly utilise the term Bátala and they still have him as the God of all that was created, and so, after the religious outsiders have come to this land to preach the faith of Jesus Christ and to baptize, they are uncertain If another name should be used for the christian god or to just use the native term Batala".

Regarding Batala and tradition, when some principal is bad, he invites his relatives for a ceremony and orders them to make a lot of food and gather fish, meat, and wine; together with all the guests they put the plated food on the floor of the house, sitting on the same floor together to eat, and then they begin the ceremony which they call manganito or maganito in their tongue, and they dance; they have the idol that they call Bátala and certain old women who they consider priestesses and old Indian Priests, they offer what they eat to the Anito and praise it in their language for the health of the sick person for whom the ceremony is performed for; After the manganito or ceremony, which usually lasts seven or eight days, they take the idols and place them in the corners of the house. According to González de Mendoza (Historia de las cosas de China, Madrid 1586) the Filipinos kept idols of men and women. "Among these, he writes, had their greatest veneration for an idol whose name was Bátala: whom they revered by tradition, as an ancient god.

Although there were also many other gods that were given great esteem. They also worshiped the sun and the moon, whose eclipses were celebrated with elaborate ceremonies called Magaduras. The aforementioned Grijalva said: "Ancient idolatry, and superstitions were present. They worshiped idols, and an all-powerful deity, and believed the soul was eternal, but that they were always reborn into mortal bodies, and so, they had a certain transmigration from one body to another; they believe that the Gods rewarded or punished them by placing them in bodies beautiful or ugly, poor or rich, good or bad, lucky or not (This was Brahmanism).

Morga says: "The supernatural beings would interact with them regularly, they would appear to them in different forms some horrible and frightening and some of fierce animals, which they feared, both trembled and adored. They would make idols of all of the supernatural beings which they would place at altars in caves and private temples, where they offered them perfumes, incense, and food they called the idols Anitos".

CHAPTER 3

THE DEVIL DOESN'T EXIST

From Deuteronomy, we find the selfish idea that only our own is the true God, and the others are the Devil, despite the fact that we are all equally children of a single Heavenly Being. The truth is that there is no such Devil. Scripture does not say that God created you, and then created the Devil. It is not possible to think that the Lord has created such a perverse being destined only to harm the human race; and if this was not his destiny, then the Creator would have made an error. The idea of Satan or Sytan is exotic, of Arab origin; Only Jobe speaks of him, the prophet Zacharias imitated the prophet Ezekiel and that of Isaiah to arbitrarily apply it to Luzbel, they are only actually referring in an express and undoubted way to the kings of Tyre and Babylon respectively you can check it in the Bible. English Romanists worship Satan or Sytan under the name of Saint Swithin, and in Poictiers, (France) they adore him in the form of a dragon with the name of Saint Vermine or Verme (Verme means worm).

All people represent foreign gods as imaginary evil Guardian's or demons, alongside the groups of fierce and frightening animals, and for this reason it is not surprising that the Filipinos painted the gods of their enemies as harmful animals or spirits and if his own idols weren't perfect either, no doubt it would be because they were not yet fully accomplished deities; but they assured, and until now reassure, that their Anitos are paragons of beauty.

The Bible, and especially the Roman novels, bring us accounts of nefarious apparitions, but there is no such thing as a Devil, this is a phenomenon of fantasy or memory, if not of epic illusion, just as we remember certain people and they appear in our dreams. The image of a seen person is printed more or less in memory, as if it were a cinematographic tape, and when in the turns of the opening takes, said image appears, and we remember it; but sometimes it is due to a mental disturbance, although not exactly by madness, which can make the affected see visions. Such experiences can be brought about by simple disturbances promoted by asterism or nerves, or by deep sadness, nostalgia, love or simply by thinking too much of a said person, sometimes we also seem to see them by illusion or imagination.

The famous French astronomer Camilo Flammarion, in an article published in 1899, in Revue des Revues, invited the public to send him accounts of apparitions seen by healthy and truthful people, to test their suspicions about the apparitions that they were some sort of transmission through brain vibrations or telepathy, and he cited one or two cases in which when concentrating his thought to a person in another room, they saw what he was thinking of at that time. But, these cases are noted as more frequent between lovers, which is explainable, because there is more passion between them. Another case that is very important to mention is that of a beautiful young woman, the sister of the rich neighbor of Manila's Mr. Faustino Lichauco, who was in Hong Kong at the time, it was his first time being away from his mother and he thought he saw her despite knowing she was in Manila. He was overcome with sadness immediately and said my mother has died from a broken heart. He was so sure of it, they had to ask if it were true by sending a cable to Manila, and they replied that she had passed.

People who fast also often can have powerful supernatural

encounters many have been evidenced by the priests of the Romanists, and this also will have happened undoubtedly through the baglanes (priests and priestesses of Anitism) as well. The friars who testified to these appearances thought they were true and authentic. Tales of apparitions and the supernatural can invoke fear and horror one may see a vision on the wall, a woman in a dress floating ; A haunting ghost, and the moans of the supernatural beings that usually suckle from their mothers in the squares of deserted and dark villages, and other sounds of woes of souls in pain. We have read cases of people who have seen their own ghost, among them the great French novelist Guy dé Maupassant; but then he also died insane. In one of his latest scientific magazines, the Madrid journalist and physician Vicente Vera gives us a summary of recent research on the subject, and he says: It is a curious thing that goblins, ghosts, or apparitions have always been represented at all times and in all countries, without color, that is to say, white. The natural explanation is that, in the vast majority of cases of people who have had these encounters in certain altered states of mind or under the influence of certain elements can experience visions, that to the individual or group they are certain it is real.

Sometimes they perceive unnatural sounds or noises, other times they see things usually without color. Many individuals in hospitals while they have had a fever, have experienced seeing specters, visions, and apparitions. When questioned about it later by the doctors, it is general to state that the visions have been similar, some having the appearance of seeing stone statues wrapped in sheets. The cases in which color is remembered in the sighting are rare. It seems, therefore, that the encounter corresponds to an imperfect impression, in effect, it gives two orders of sensations: that of the intensity of light and colors.

In the case of the specters, for whatever reason the brain cannot perfectly process the experience or encounter.

Probably because the medulla and optic nerve in which it occurs is subjective to the sensation of colors. This same effect can also be obtained by administering certain substances to the individual susceptible to hallucinations. Altered visions and colors can be produced with Indian hashish or hemp; blue with alcohol; red with atropine, duboisin, scopolamine, quinine and excessive use of tobacco; and yellow sensations can be achieved with acids picric and salicylic, with digitalis and phenacetin, with external application of chromic acid and iodoform and with inhalations of carbon oxide. The bite of the viper also gives yellow sensations. The Mexican mezcal, a spirit drink obtained by fermenting and subsequently distilling the juice of various plants from the genus cacti, produces visions of various simultaneous colors.

CHAPTER 4

BATHALA & MAYKAPAL

Morga in his chronicles writes about the Filipino beliefs stating: "they adored the sun and the moon making traditions, ceremonies and rituals to the celestial bodies. they also adored a Bird that is painted on the mountains yellow which is called Bathala. Another animal that is given great reverence is the crocodile, when they see crocodiles, they drop to their knees to placate them. Most temples or places of worship were located within or close proximity to the residence of their elders.

There was no ceremonial circumcision, but shamans and priestesses would give prayers and conduct ceremonies for the sick. They believed in the afterlife and heroes would be given great rewards for their acts, but they did not believe in hell. Some buried their dead in their own homes having their bodies and bones for a long time after death and venerating their deceased family members as if they were living and present." According to the Jesuit Quirino, "The Filipinos did not use their writing system to preserve their religion, but only for correspondence and record keeping. Thus, nothing written on the matter was found and everything that has been known is based on the traditions being passed on to the next generation, preserved in ceremony and in some songs that they have memorized by heart and repeat in their ocean navigations to the beat of the oar and in their rejoicing, festivals, funerals which sometimes have choirs, when many attend. In these songs they tell the fabulous genealogies and various deeds of their heroes and gods." Quirino continues: "There was one chief superior to all whom the Tagalogs call

Bathala or Maykapal, which means the maker or maker god and in the Visayas they called this entity Laon which denoted antiquity. Some songs told stories regarding the creation of the world, the beginning of the human lineage, the flood, glory, sorrow and other supernatural things, recounting thousands of stories, some in one way and others in another. One of the stories is that the first man and the first woman came out of a reed stem that burst open. So, the gods they litigated about marrying the two, due to the issue that they were related which to the gods was prohibited, but they decided to only allow it once for the necessity of the propagation of man."

The Jesuit Colin (who in the preface of his Lavor Evangélica Madrid 1663) confesses to having taken his account from Quirino and indeed he copies it literally almost exactly, however he expands on the cosmogony by putting somethings that were possibly of his own creation, as it seems to us he may have warped the original text although the sensible thing would have been that they copied it literally and that it then continued in turn with Gaspar de San Agustin, Francisco de San Antonio, Moya, Marsden, (History of Sumatra) and Lubbock. In the case of Father Colin, he may have elaborated in order to preserve The Philippine cosmogony, to prove the plausibility of Genesis, and his references regarding the giant blue bird (who in his capacity related as ominous was also called Bathala) was probably in relation to the Bathala, Maykapal, or creator God of Filipinos. Furthermore he wrote this about the Filipino cosmogony: "The world began with only heaven and water and among them a Great Bird called Maykapal(the dove, Holy Spirit of the Romanists) fluttered its wings vigorously looking for somewhere to land and not finding it, The Bird stirred the water until the waves became very high, The sky became concerned by the rising waves that they would spill over into the heavens. The sky, to appease the Bird, gave it many islands so it could have a place to land and rest. After the great bird had landed to rest, the ocean waves threw a reed ashore at its feet and Maykapal pecked them open, and a man came out from one end and a woman from the other. Although, because they were of the same bloodline some difficulties could have arose from thir first generation offspring the gods were not initially convinced on them being allowed to marry and procreate, but on the advice of the fish and the birds and one of their gods: the thundering one, dispensed them of thier concerns (Father Saint Augustine adds that it is called Linog; in Tiruray it is effectively Limog) and married them so they had many children. The father, eventually grew tired of feeding them without gain or gratitude, as many of the descendants were ungrateful and unruly so Limog took a stick and gestured to punish them for their pranks and behavior in hopes that they would develop on thier own and provide for themselves. The Children frightened by the thundering one fled and went to hide, some in the cabinets of the house and these ones were later the main people; others escaped outside of the house, and the free ones escaped altogether; those who hid in the house in the kitchen, have been here in the Philippines ever since, and those whom went outside of the house and in faraway parts, are now considered outsiders or foreigners. In Moya's account: "those who escaped altogether went inside the Earth to live in the region of fire". Fr. Quirino says, "The Tagalogs worshiped a blue bird the size of a thrush and called it Bathala, which was among them the name of divinity". Bathala, according to the Kapampangan Dictionary of P. Beivgaño, 1860, is: "A bird in which the Kapampangan's have as their water carriers". In the current traditions of the Filipinos there is no tradition that birds have been worshiped as God, but more as an ominous supernatural being. According to the signs that Quirino gives, the Bathala is the same as Salaksak of the Ilocanos, The bird of omens. The word Bathara in Sanskrit (sacred language of the indus) means 'Lord.' The Bataks of Sumatra, the Bugis and Makassar call their god Bathara Guru (master lord) which was the nickname of Shiva the third person of the Brahmanic trimurti. A Hebrew, upon hearing the word Bathala, told us that it is the same as Bethel, house of God or of El, God of the Semites, by another name Allah, so that Bathala becomes the house or incarnation of Allah. In Genesis XCI 8; XIII, The Christian god was also called Batala, according to the Relacion of 1572. We believe that the true name of the Creator God among the Tagalogs was Maykapal, and not Bathala, even only six years ago the name Bathala was not used, until it was popularized again by the Filipinos when they learned from these lightly written Chronicles that the Filipino God was called Bathala. Moreover, the Tagalogs did not even remember the word Bathala or Batala. If they really want to use this name it should be Badhala, noting that the Spanish always pronounce the letter d at the final syllable as a t. In the old Tagalog Dictionary of Fr. Noceda(year 1754) Badhala is spelled that way. Today's Tagalogs call comets or other stars that predict some event Badhala, because the ominous birds have been called Badhala. The Dayaks of Borneo call their god Mahatara (from maha, grande, and Bathará) The great lord. Perhaps the Guru corresponds to the Gugurang of the Bicolano's. We believe that the name Bathala or Badhala was only used among Filipinos who had relationships with Malaysians, Hindus or Mohammedans, which are from Southern Manila. In the North of Luzon this name is not known and has a different meaning altogether something like that of a lord, like Panginoon's treatment or Apo, but from the north to south all Filipinos have The Anito's or Ancient One's, at the same time which meant Ancestor. Bathala, then, was a generic title for myths, extended to ominous birds, comets and other fabulous beings that they revered. So now there is Badhala, Maykapal, Lord Creator, Badhala Katutubo, and Anito. It is known; the ancient Visayas called the images of their Diuatas generally Bathala and the Bicolano's also spoke of a "Bathala that was an Anito that made those who accompanied them happy and prevented disasters from happening to them". It will be the same for Katutobo. Quirino continues: " They recognized invisible spirits, another life or afterlife and demons, who could tremble the earth in extreme instances. Their idolatry is to worship and have their Ancestors for Gods, particularly men who were appointed, brave, virtuous and wise, as seen today among the people of the mountains. They attributed divinity to their elders such as thier father when he died, and the old men themselves died with honor in all of his actions, with seriousness, and divinity. They were buried in designated places in memory of them, they had little Idols made of stone, wood, bone, ivory or crocodile skulls and teeth, sacrifices to these Idols would be offered for their needs in the afterlife and also made for the delivery of blessings to the living family members. They also worshiped animals, birds, the sun, the moon, and especially the arch of the sky or firmament which they attributed to their way of divinity. Alligators and crocodiles received a great degree of veneration; they called them Nono (grandparent) or lolong, they gave him offerings that they carried in their boats and asked for blessings and safe passage. They also worshiped A dark bird called Meylupa, or owner of the land.

There was no old tree to which they did not attribute great divinity, it was sacrilegious to think of cutting one down. They worshiped on stones, rocks, pits, caves and certain points along the sea or river, putting water on them at those points in water ceremonies. On the Manila River there was a large stone temple that for many years was sacred until it was torn down by the Augustinians, replaced with a cross and the chapel of San Nicolás de Tolentino, In Panay there was another point called Nasso going to Potol where many plates of offerings were seen in it daily. Another custom was that If they saw a snake, lizard or heard sneezing they turned away from it. In Taytay many houses had their own temple the size of a turret carved with many different symbols and motifs , to which they also passed through an intricate door into a sacred place dedicated to the Anito, although there we were not able to witness their ceremonies. In some places the temples were painted such as in the Visayas were I found at the entrance of the town a small box with only the roof and mezzanine, that served as a place of sacrifice. In Mindanao I saw many houses with Andites and in them Anitos and a pot with coals and incense, each home had their own Anito. The priests are called in Tagalog Katolonan and in The Visayas Babaylan. The supernatural beings spoke to them in their sacrifices and the Anitos represented the ancient ones or ancestors whom they worshiped. In one ceremony The Katolonan or Babaylan, dancing to the sound of the drum or bell, and doing various rituals for a wounded or ill person would sacrifice a pig or hen and then would give an oracle about what they wanted to know. The Babaylan would always be given the best part of the sacrificed animal and they were also paid in cotton, gold or chickens. Priestly status was achieved, when an Anito directly chose an individual through oracles, it could also be inherited by blood or through apprenticeship.

CHAPTER 5
ANITISMO

The True Original Religion of The Philippines, like that of that of all Malays is the cult of the souls of the Ancient Ones or Ancestors, which they called Anitos, which etymologically derives from the root word Ani (peri-spirit, shadow or semi-spiritual soul) and hantu (Sanskrit for dead or death). According to Fr. Aduarte: "there was a good year and a bad year", And as already we have said, good was the soul of an ancestor, and the bad was that of an enemy. Originally from Mindanao to the extreme North of Luzon the deified souls were called Anitos; but with the arrival of the Hindus, they began to be called diuatas in the Visayas and Mindanao islands; in Manila and the surrounding areas, badhala's. In Camarines, between the Visayas and the Luzónicos, they were called indistinctly Anitos or diuatas or just souls of the ancestors. According to Father Colin, "The idols here represent the ancestors, the Tagalogs called them Anito and the Visayas diuatas. There were Anitos of the mountains, fields, farms and more, from whom they asked permission to pass or enter that area, and to whom they entrusted their crops and they asked for the fertility of their fields, There was an Anito of the ocean and waters, protector of their fisheries and navigations, an Anito of the home to whom the child was entrusted to at birth. Growing up the Anito would be invoked to protect and guide them in their labors, difficulties and dangers. The Filipinos maintain the belief that the sea is sacred and everyone who dies in it will go to the place of happiness. Undoubtedly, these drowned souls would be the ones Later they turned into the Anitos of the waters: good, if they were from grandparents, and harmful, if they were from enemies.

CHAPTER 6

PARADISE

For both the ancient and contemporary Filipinos that call the mountainous regions home, they believed that the righteous, those who lived without sin, and the brave went to a Paradise, which was usually located at the top of a sacred mountain in the vicinity of their region and therefore varied according to the province. Some of the names for paradise and places to enter were: Mákang for the Tagalogs Kaluwalhatian (place of delights), in the Visayas Ologan pointing to Mount Madías of Iloiloin particular, the Bicolano's had Kamburagan or Kamutauayan, for the Kianganes it was located in the Kadungayan forest, the tribes of Abra pointed to the mountains venerable in its vicinity, the Bagobos the Pangulili and the Tirurays call Bongo the resting place. According to the Bible, Paradise was indeed found on a mountain, Ezekiel 28:14 You were anointed as a guardian cherub, for I had ordained you, on the holy mountain of God; where you walked among the fiery stones. Isaiah 14:13 I will preside on the mountain of the gods far away in the north. Even Jesus assured the following: "And no man hath ascended up to heaven, that did not come down from heaven" Gospel of Saint John 3:13. All of which seems to confirm that God in his infinite mercy, will not want to distance the deceased from their living relatives, so he places them close to them to protect them against adversity.

There would be no true glory for a good mother to be away from her children; there would be no greater happiness for her than the one she would experience If the Creator would allow her to always be close to them to love them and to defend them from dangers and setbacks, And what we say about the mother, it extends to anyone with the natural desire of a mother, to continue living with one's relatives and friends in the afterlife. Blumentritt says that those in Cebu, Bohol and Bantayan located their Paradise on a mountain in Borneo, and This is why he supposes that they came from there, since the Malays and Filipinos usually designate their Paradise at the points of thier providence According to Quirino, on some islands they believed that no woman could be saved who had a husband, until he came in the other life to take her hand at a certain passage of a river because she had as her only bridge a narrow wood, which has to be crossed to go to the resting place they called Kaluwalhatian. According to Aduarte, the Filipinos believed that when the body died, the soul went to a river or lagoon, where there was a boat with an elderly captain or psychopomp, and to pay the fare for boarding, the family tied money to the arm of the corpse and to make sure the ferryman would stop for the women they painted their hands black. He would escort the souls to some very beautiful fields where love was abundant and a very pleasant life passed, eating, drinking and enjoying themselves until they came again into this world. According to Blumerítritt, the Higuecina or Igueines believed that The Psychopomp Anito was named Maguayaw, and he carried the souls in his balañgay (boat) to another life. Others called this figure Pandakesita. Regarding this topic, we have stories from Ilocos that in the middle of the sea there is an island of snakes and when the Elders became very old, they moved them from the island of Luzon to The Island of Snakes and there they turned into stones. What Aduarte says is: "The Filipinos used to bury their dead with their weapons, instruments and regalia, and they put them in coffins in the shape of a boat, to use it in the afterlife, since they believed that the other life was very similar to the present. The Europeans have this belief as well and call it the boat of Caron. According to P. Villaverde in his report published In the Courier Sino Annamita of 1879, the people of the Kiangan mountains designate the stars and planets, especially the sun, as the abodes of Gods" We could not check if it is true or not; but some from those same mountains indicated to us that Kadungayan mountain is the location of paradise, which seems contrary to what Villaverde said. We believe that the true location of paradise for Filipinos is located in the mountains, not the stars. The stars were lamps hanging in the celestial vault, they do not journey there in the afterlife. The Bulalakaweño's of Paragua, point out that the abode of the gods or invisible Guardian's is in the stars. Also, the Ilocanos and Tagalogs point it out as the abode of the Katatawean or the fabulous bird. Langit means sky, that blue space that we see over our heads; but it was not the place of paradise for the ancient Filipinos.

CHAPTER 7

NO HELL IN THE PHILIPPINES

According to San Augustin, the Visayans called the place of Sorrow: Sulad and according to San Antonio they called it Kasanaan. The Anito Pandakesita or Maguayaw brings the Souls to Sulad and when the proper rituals, ceremonies, and sacrifices are performed by the Babaylans, the soul can rise from Sulad to Paradise. The Filipino Sulad is a much better place than the western ideal of purgatory. According to Blumentritt, Pandakesita, may be a traditional Filipino word that was Castilianized, it is probably composed of Pandak (dwarf, duwende, or Kukü of the mandayas) and of Sitan, which is what the Muslims call Satan. It is clear that the idea of Hell is not a Filipino one, but it still is an important concept. The Bagobos of Mindanao say Hell is located at the volcano Apo and the Tagbanua of Paragua consider Hell to be located at Basaud, but the Filipinos do not have a word corresponding to Hell. The Sulad of the Bisaya's is probably the closest idea to Hell in The Philippines. With that in mind Let's believe then that the Filipinos are just like the Malay's of Borneo, our neighbors and brothers that did not have a belief in Hell and considered God incapable of teaching or punishing a dead man, and that the continuous misery and struggles of this life was punishment enough for our sins.

CHAPTER 8
ORDER OF THE SONAT

According to San Antonio, the ancient Filipinos had a religious leader similar to the catholic bishop or pope, which in Tagalog they called "Sonat" whom they all revered as one who could forgive sins and also could ordain other priests and priestesses, they had supreme authority of the priestly class and could provide salvation or damnation to all peoples. This position was among the most important and honored in thier communities and a great reverence was given to them. W. Retana suffered an error in assuming that the Sonat was a circumciser, as the Pr. Martínez de Zúñiga and Noceda had also been mistaken when they assumed etymologically that the Sonat meant to circumcise or cut or that it pertained to a similar ritual involving young men, maidens and girls. In the Philippines male circumcision was performed but for hygienic purposes and is called tuli or turi or pag tutuli, and is the same regarding the cutting or removal of something from the female, woman or animal. In some cases it was performed so that the individual didnt feel lust, in that case you say bating, in Tagalog. The ancient Tagalog's spoke also of a mamamating tawo, sorcerer or healer, and seems to be the one designated as the circumciser of women. According to Morga the act or ceremony of circumcision was sacred. Although some believe this practice was Mohammedan in origin and not Filipino. Filipino priests, according to their merits, were consecrated into the cult of the Ancestors and they were indoctrinated into different sects and categories, being the prelate they often became the ones who made the sacrifices to the Creators or to the Anitos. In Zambales Bayok was called the chief among the priests. This Bayok was in charge of the cult of Malyari, the supreme god of Zambales, (similar to Maykapal) he was the one who has power, the owner or creator of everything. It was his oracle or prophecy that held the mos weight amongst the people, and was the one who created all of the other beings. In the Visayas, it seems that they also had their own bishops; their sect was mentioned in 1673 they even had Pope's as well like the Tagalog Sonat, such as some of the recent ones like Pope Isio and others. At the time of the Spanish Conquest, the Bohol Babaylan was very important and powerful They were renowned for their prophecies, healing, and magic. The Babaylans in one ritual had a decorated garment they wore that was adorned with gold, they were rich and powerful as wel and controlled the mines of that island. The Spanish chroniclers reported that, it has been witnessed that the upper class of the priestly hierarchies was reserved for "chosen ones" and others that were the most deserving. The Spanish accounts that stated they were men who dressed as women were incorrect, they would wear plain garments that to the Spaniards would resemble feminine skirts, as the Roman priests garments would have appear to outsiders also, they were religious garments similar to the Catholic chasuble, let us bear in mind that the first Spaniards in the islands found the Filipino's already as an advanced civilization in some places and tribalistic in other provinces just as they are now in the province and in the mountain tribes of the Aetas and Igorot's along the coasts. Those precolonial large towns and cities were often as civilized as they are today in modern times. They were not uncivilized tribes, but cultures already developed. One of these cities to the extreme of Luzon, for example called Lawag (Ilocos Norte) was already a city of forty thousand people, there were many other large towns and cities in that region although Lawag did have the largest population.

In pre-colonial Manila they had stone walls and even cannons long before the arrival of the Spaniards. Filipinos had kings who maintained diplomatic relations with neighboring countries; they owned large ships that reached Borneo and other Malay islands; they had beautiful sophisticated clothing and textiles, some made of silk; they had their own writing, and they ate on plates imported from China. The Philippines was already a well advanced civilization.

The Filipino priests, such as the baglanes of the Itnegs were the most respectable in the towns for their exemplary conduct; They were not like certain priests and Pharisees who under the pretext of long prayers, limited themselves to emptying the pockets of their followers but they were more similar to the apostles constituted to Jesus Christ, they moralized the peoples with their preaching, preserving the purity of culture and customs. They also put limits on the excesses of their perspective communities indulgences and parties. According to one chronicler noted, "if the noise went beyond the limits of prudence, the Bayok threw on their heads a little of dust, bran or sand and as by magic the order was reestablished". The priests and priestesses, more than in their ceremonies, put their greatest concentration and care in curing the sick and tormented with massage, oils and medicinal plants. Their healing powers and effectiveness of their medicine was renowned throughout the islands and admired greatly by the people. The proper medicinal plants and recipes for the proper illness were only known by them. We could list numerous cases that were ruled incurable by the Spanishbrewing the Hospital of Manila. When the patients were discharged by Spanish doctors, they were easily cured by The Filipino Priests and Priestesses.

CHAPTER 9
CEREMONIES

In addition to those aformentioned, there were other cultural ceremonies, such as when the Itnegs give their children their names, they take them to a forest accompanied by a Shaman and others of the priestly class. When they reach the shade of the chosen tree, The Minister of the Anito approaches with a machete (bolo) and having the neophyte close, he solemnly says: Your name is ... (the first name chosen), unloading a blow on the trunk. If the tree bleeds, that is the child's name; but if not, they will strike it again and announce another name until the tree bleeds. This ceremony is still preserved in the mountains of Abra. It is a genuine Filipino one. In Ilocos they keep a similar ritual unloading the machete on the back of a plate of wood and they call it buniag ti sirok ti latok. With this ceremony they change the name to remedy an affliction, The Aztecs have a god they call upon to remedy afflictions peculiarly with a similar name called Tlaloc.

Among the ancient Zambales, the neophyte wore her hair down, from which hung a few small golden ornaments and stood on a high stone surrounded by relatives and friends. After some ceremonies, the Bayok spilled the blood of a slaughtered pig on the head of the one to be blessed and then cut off the ends of her hair, they then threw the thin ornaments of gold into the crowd that were snatched away by those present with a cacophony of shouts, music and songs.

In Mindanao, Basilan the samales-laut or "sea gypsies" also have a similar "christening" ritual called Gunting. Purification by captivity, another ceremony imitated or similar to baptism. A principal who had fallen captive, he could not return to his town without first having been purified. They usually would be bathed in some river, stream or sea, and afterwards the babaylan, dressed in thier special ornaments would begin performing some rites, splitting a coconut and throwing the broth and an egg yolk on the captive's head. Later, he returned to bathe and then was ready to be received by his family and friends with joy, which translated into a banquet. We assume that this purification ceremony obeyed customs to which the ancient Filipinos and Japanese considered to be dishonored for example a coward who falls into the power of the enemy alive.

Regarding Weddings and other festivities banquets, dances and music usually started in the morning and went into the evening. The priestess, dancing to the music, sacrificed a pig. She then presented a plate full of uncooked rice, on top she joined the bride and groom's hands and with a deafening howl she celebrated the marriage. Roast the pig already, they prepared the food. Most of the tables were low for example dulang diners sat on the floor and the bride and groom together with thier godmothers. The bride and groom ate from the same plate and drank from a single glass. Their godmothers assisted them and taught them the duties and hygiene of the married. The Attendees celebrated with laughter regarding the significant teachings of the godmothers. The priestess extolled the marriage and ended by asking for the bride and groom an offering (bigay kaya) and also from the attendants, which she gathered on a plate. The guests left taking a few grains of rice served at the wedding ceremony. If they were slaves, the ceremony was reduced and the bride and groom would simply drink from the same tabo and give a cry.

CHAPTER 10

THE AETA: GODS OF THE MOUNTAINS

While keeping in mind all of the historical facts we have covered up to this point. We are now going to explore the different regions from North to South and you will soon see that as we approach the Southern Island of Mindanao which is the point of origin or place of entrance of the Hindus and Mohammedans into the Philippines it will become clear how those religions heavily influenced the original religion of The Philippines. First, we will explore the theogony of The Aeta who seem to be the aborigines or most ancient and original people of the whole world, (perhaps they are the missing link many have sought after between man and its ancient ancestors), they belong to the most Ancient Animists. To be clear animism and not fetishism. As it stands it seems the evidence is clear that Fetishism did not come before Animism. Unfortunately, there is not much early writing from the Spanish about The Aeta, but the accounts we do have from Spanish missionaries states that whatever religion they did have was not shared with them or other outsiders, so most of the Spanish accounts are based on mere conjecture. Although from what we know now, it Looks like Undoubtedly, they worshiped the dead. They closed and protected the graves of their ancestors and warned neighboring tribes of the burial sites, so that they do not unconsciously desecrate them. In some cases, death or banishment would be the punishment for such an act. The Cagayan Aeta believe that the souls go into the forest in the afterlife and that is where they can find paradise. Also, when they slaughter an animal for food, sale, or trade they will cut off a slice and throw it to the sky saying "this is for you" according to Father Villaverde. There are similar rituals followed in Ilocos and among the Tagalogs that they call pasinaya (first fruits). The Aeta of Camarines Norte bury the corpse of their ancestors under their house and then move from that land. That is why they stay in each place for only a brief time and live like nomads. The Aeta that are designated superior or most admirable, are put into coffins and they are buried directly under sacred trees; they are also very superstitious, for example: The women are the ones who build their houses, believing that if men built them, it would be bad luck.

The Aeta of Camarines told Father Castaño: That there was a great god of the sky, that it was the one who thunders and commands the things that cause fear on the earth. When they died, they walked wandering through the meadows to the forests, appearing frequently at night, until they disappeared from this world to go dwell in another place eternally. According to Ang Sugba (journal) of Cebu, the Aeta there call God Mahana; but we are not sure, since neither Mr. A.B. Meyer, who studied the Aeta in depth, nor the seven foreign authors who provided him with data, noted an Aeta word corresponding to God. Mahana possibly comes from the Bisaya word paggama (to create)? Or Manama the powerful god of the Bagobo (people of the mountain). The Aeta of Dumagats, located on the NE coast of Luzon, speak of Balendik, a demon with skinny legs, whitish color and the head of a horse. So, while for most this demon is black, according to them it is white. According to the English doctor Mundt-Lauff, the Aeta of the Philippines like those of the Moluccas worship the sun god Bof and keep a bonfire in its honor at night, considering it a great sin to spit on the fire. We have not been able to verify if it is true or not. The Aeta of Angat are said to have magical talismans and powerful potions; one is a love potion called manibig, made from the amatoria plant. Some Aeta mestizos from the mountains of Sibul (Bulacan) have told me that they call God Maykadapat, a Kapampangan term that means creator, equivalent to Maykapal and that when they ask for his protection in cases of danger, they say: "Oh bubo Maykadapat pantungoan"(Oh grandparent Maykadapat, save us).

They bury their dead with their regalia, weapons and instruments, so as not to see them as painful memories, and then they leave the place. It is forbidden to approach their graves so as not to disrespect their burial. They say that in the woods you can hear them, but they are invisible. Sometimes they knock down trees, roll large stones, and drag or carry reeds (bamboos), etc. They are the souls of some of the dead. They do not believe in hell or a place where souls are burned or punished. In the Aeta pantheon: The sun is called synag, moon guimerá, star bituin, thunder tukoddol, lightning tokelat, rain dussok, soul multó or tumánod, father tigama, and mother tigna. The Aeta have told me directly that the soul of the dead is called Anito and that they do not dare to look at them or it will cause horror. I would be extraordinarily grateful if my countrymen from Zambales, Mariveles, Ilocos, etc. would also study, research, and write directly about the beliefs and superstitions of The Aeta and the other Tribes of the Mountains.

CHAPTER 11

A GOD IS BURIED ON KABUNIAN MOUNTAIN

The Religion of the Igorot's is also based on the cult of the ancient ones. The supreme Anito of the different tribes of the Igorot's of Luzon (Apayaos, Guinaangs, Ifugaos and other denominations) is Kabunían, without a doubt he is the same as Buni that according to the Ilocano Dictionary of P. Carro, (1849), is the god of the mountains, and according to another author, Buni is the supreme god of the Kiangan Mountains. Kabunían is capable of annihilating everything created, even nature itself, and when it thunders, they believe that he is angry, and to appease him, they sacrifice a pig. He is their god of war and of peace. Now, Kabunian was also known as a famous warrior, whose burial is still marked on the mountain that bears his name in the vicinity of the Bakun river that joins the Amburayan of Ilocos.

Sinibaldo de Mas wrote in 1843: "In the afternoon I visited the Bacun cemetery, which is at the edge of the town along the river; I found twenty-four pine plank coffins hanging in the air, at the site there were Sculptures of a Carabao and a Pig; they called these cemeteries Luddut. At this site there was a temple and at the top I saw embedded into the wall the tomb of an ancient King of Bacun. I don't know how they could have gotten there, unless it was created by craftsmen. We then went up to the opposite mountain range, and we followed the treacherous path until about nine o'clock, when we began to climb the high mountain called Kabunían that derives its name from a God, this mountain seemed to be made of living stone, it was the most dangerous I have ever seen; We had to make holes in the stone to put, and hold our feet and then push one another up. At one o'clock in the afternoon we managed to reach the high summit, in which there is a sacred tomb that the Igorot's claim to be their God Kabunian. 'Report *on the Philippine Islands.*

Other historians say that the Supreme God of the Igorot's is called Apo; but this word means lord and grandparent and is therefore associated sometimes with Kabunían and other Saints. Kabunían was said to have a wife named Bangan and they had two sons Lumáoig or Lumawid and Kabigat, and two daughters Daunguen and Bugan, the siblings married each other, which put the human race in danger. According to some, Bugan is the daughter of the god Apo and wife of Mananahahut the God of the Sun, and main Anito of the Kianganes. In this case, Mananahahut is the same as Kabigat, The Anito of the Igorot's of Mamut and the Alta- bañes (central Luzon). But Apo, in addition to Bugan, has another son, Uban who may be the same as Iban, which we will talk about. Among the many Mountain tribes of Luzon, they believe that they are the direct descendants of the gods, and that is why they have many different names for their deities depending on the tribe because their ancestors name was that of the deity. It was a similar system to that which is found in ancient India, Egypt and elsewhere, when two tribes or cultures were unified through marriage or treaty, the gods of those people would also become connected through rites and ceremonies. Thus Mananahahut, the supreme Anito of the Kianganes, appears as Apo's son-in-law; and the main saint of the Igorot's of Lepanto, Lumaoig appears as the son of Apo Kabunían.

Abra's Tingguians say that there are two main Anito's a good Anito Alan (Adan) and another bad one, Apat And many other lesser or demigod Anito's, which, according to the ranchero's, are named: Misi, Dasiasoias, Balitok (gold), Líniantakaw, Banheis, Dalít, Sipat, Sadibubu, Salanga and others. Undoubtedly, the pantheon was polytheistic or at the minimum had at its origins polytheism; but the prevailing idea of Kabunian absorbs and makes the name of God their own, the one who proved themself endowed with the most power. They considered that as the supreme God and when they speak of God, they say: "Our God "and not "our Anito's ". They allude to a single Anito, as the Bagobo's, Tíruray's and Súbano's of Mindanao who speak of a single Diwata; confirming what the friar chroniclers said that the Filipinos were already monotheists at the time of the arrival of the Spanish. They all agree that this supreme Anito is the creator and that he was an ancestor of extraordinary power and prowess. The Gaddan's call their supreme Anito Amanolay, the creator of man and is also known as the bear of Dalingay. The tribes at the mountains of the Agno River invoke Kaspek and Magsip, children of the sun, in their ceremonies to cure illnesses. And who is this anito of the sun? Is it Mananahut, lord of the sun, or is it that Agno which came from Agni, God of fire for the Hindus? other gods of different Igorot's are Limoan, Libongan and Libugon of the Ifugaos; Tibagon, Bovang (Baliti's idol). Pati, anito of the rain of the Ifugaos, perhaps it is the same Si-Pat Pati in Sanskrit which means lord; the Hindus call Vishnu Sri Pati. Also, the Tagalog's worshiped Lakan (lord) Pati as protector of their fields.

The Ifugaos also have an Anito named Sanian reminiscent of the Sangiang, Guardian Anito of the Dayaks from Borneo. The gods of the enemy tribes would be considered evil spirits; but for their own tribe the gods were of course good, this was also the case in India, Egypt, Persia, and elsewhere. A good example of this is Nagbuyagan, who is a powerful Anito for the Igorot's and Ifugaos but is a destroying demon for the Itnegs. He is capable of destroying men and other gods, except Kabunian, who was another famous warrior god.

The Igorot's of the Kiangan speak of evil Guardian's they call Karangat. The Katalanganes have Anito's called

Sialó and Tchiehonan and are goddesses, which were their wives Binalinga and Bebenangan respectively: which are reminiscent of Bangan. The Igorot's and Guinaanes have the Sulit bird which brings prophecies, and the kíring or kiling, a small bird that has a large neck like that of the argentine bird and when it sings a specific song it heralds the next hurricane. The Igorot's of Kagubatan (Lepanto) believe that the souls of their ancestors are incarnated in the eels found at a waterfall at the location of a sacred cave, They feed them, saying: "Eel come here [dalit], Eel, take this offering of food, bring me luck, grant me good health, and protect me from disease." The same Eel worship and belief is found in those of southern Sulawesi and those of Amboina. The Mandayas believe a fabulous Eel Deity, called the Kasilig, surrounds the world, and when the Kagang crab bites its tail, it shakes the world causing an earthquake. After reading about the above-mentioned in a published article, I traveled to Benguet, and among the Igorot's of those luscious mountains and some from Bontok, I read that article to them, in their native language, I hardly got through the first line before they tried to contradict that story.

They stated that now they believe in only one God, called Kabunían and similar to that of the Christian God, as the creator, most powerful and superior to everything. They unanimously assured me: you Christians call it God, here it is Kabunían, in the whole world there is only one God for all nations. The diversity of names is only because of the difference in languages and traditions; but deep down our religion is the same as the Christian. In this notion, they undoubtedly believe theirs are better than those of mine is an ideal exclusive to Christians. It is inaccurate, they added that we worship many gods. Only Kabunían is God; the others we venerate were wise, powerful men; they're like your saints. Neither do we worship in trees, nor in the sun. One of thier wisemen has told me: God is a powerful man who is not man, he is one for all. "If he's not a man, what is he then?". "A being superior to all." Another, narrowed the definition replying: "It was a man, but a very extraordinary man, as he is the one who made everything we see, wise, powerful, the one who existed before all things and the one who directs everything. (They are fatalistic). They agree that Kabunian is not a man, but only because he does not know how to define a rational Being who is not a man.

However from this modern idea of them, there is remains of his anthropomorphism, since they say that Kabunian appears in the form of an Igorot and disappears; sowed in the fields of Bontok land that they now consider sacred, a handful of rice that yielded enough harvest to support a whole family or house, and also some other groups they call him Aba. To Kabunian, some give the title of Apo; this is the Ilocano word for Lord; but the word Lord does not exist among the Igorot's. This ideal was the same in the mountains of Sibul, that is, all men are equal. Apo, in Igorot it means only grandparent, and it is also improper, because Kabunían was not an ancestor.

This is what an enlightened Igorot told me. Do you know a giant god like Angngaló of the Ilocano's? I asked them, 'No," they replied. But Kabunían, to be able to make heaven, he must have been a very tall being. Yes, 'very tall, one answered me. According to another, A god one day turned the world upside down, that is, the top came down, and vice versa, erasing all of humanity, except for two siblings, who married to each other, and renewed the human race. But an Igorot educated by the Christians, interrupted: That is the flood of the Christians that our grandparents heard; more, it is not ours, like neither did Iban and Adan, the first men, according to those traditions.

One from Bontok assured me: Kabunían had two children, the male (Batanga) and a female Bángan. They married and fathered two twins, one for each breast: boy and girl.

These were the parents of coughs that go with loincloths, and that is the Igorot's. When these grew, the first family produced two other twins, a boy (Ari) and a girl (Aran) and they were sent to Ilocos to speak with Kabunian regarding the commissioning of weapons manufacturing technology and currency development ,but more specifically firearms, The Ilocano's, therefore, were the inventors of the gun and currency, according to them. Thus, they procreated two by two, and were the fathers of the various nations of the earth.

The names of the first people, as well as the beliefs, vary according to the dialects and rancherias. The Bontok they say that Batanga their first man, is the same as Lumnaoig, but those of Benguet pronounce it Dumagüíd. They suppose that he is different from Batanga, mong the first men, those of Bontok cite Ali or Ari, which means king; and Inaldawan, by another name, Aguew, the sun and owner of snakes and eels. The women were Bángan, Bugan; but they do not know Daungen, who must be Dúgay. Otan also to Aran or Adam and two they went, and that they must be Adam and Eve; but it is worth noting that the first woman, according to the Ilocanos, was called Aran. They do not know of Ángngaló or a tradition similar to the Ilocano cosmogony, but some mention Ali or Ari (king), who must be the gigantic King of creation of the Tagalog's. The Igorot's are not certain of the sexes they do not think that such a character is male or female, nor do they know who formed each.

According to those of Bontok, the dead go to the mountain, the place of the Igorot's when they die, they went to the country of the Ifugao's place of heat; and when the Ilocanos die to the cold region of the Igorot's. An educated Igorot from Benguet, contradicts the stories given by those from Bontok, stating: The first men were not children of Kabunían, which were demi-gods; but that they were extraordinary men, wise men, doctors, powerful, and that is why in our kañaw (ceremonies or prayers for healing), we invoke them, for that is how we were entrusted, so that we may be cured. One of the oldest stories was relayed like this:

The women priestesses like Bángan, Búgan, Dügay and Kodíwan the Great were shamans, capable of resuscitating the dead and healing wounds. Kabunian made the first men: the Igorot's of earth, and the Chinese of carabao bones. It is ancient and general in the country the saying that the unfriendly races were formed from the remnants of particular animals. The black people were made at night and whites by day and he distributed them on the earth. Before the sky was low; and when towering trees grew, Kabunían lifted them up. Then the moon was even brighter than the sun Kabunían requisitioned the provisions that each requested for sacrifice, the sun requested the flesh and bones of animals; but it was the moon that desire the flesh and bones of man, for which Kabunían punished her by diminishing her clarity, covering her eyes with mud.

Those of Bontok have a different tale and say that envious the sun of the moon, he blinded her with mud: from that act we can thank for the darkness of the night, for the Igorot's, then, the moon is a demon or an evil entity. When there is a dead person, they set out to see a man on the moon who they think appears on its surface and when the satellite appears on the horizon as a great disk of fire, they assume very bad intentions and then insult him with dishonest words, as if he were a man. Just as an Igorot supposes that the sun is female.

Dúgay, invited by Dumagüíd, tried to go up to heaven to see Kabunían; but died after being scorched by the sun; this is how they discovered that it is fire In Benguet, the sun is sekict, the moon is bulan, and the sky is akú. They do not cry out in eclipses, nor do they believe that the sun or the moon are devoured by some dragon, and they only invoke Kabunían to restore their clarity, as they fearfully invoke him in tremors. Only among certain tribes is the saying that a fabulous animal moves the earth in earthquakes. The rainbow is not a bridge to the sky, but a sign that there is rain. "It goes to look for fish in the river, when it appears," they say. And perhaps this is a metaphor to imply that fish abound when the rains move the rivers.

Burials: They bury their dead seated with all their utensils, under their houses, except the rich who they entomb into some rock formation. If they dream that the deceased has been with them, they bury them again with new offerings. They take a long time to bury their corpses after death, only until after they have slaughtered a certain number of animals and performed the proper ceremonies.

According to those of Benguet, the souls of the dead go to the Pulag an unknown region of the earth where they gather. When a dead man arrives, many come out to receive him. He who commits suicide by hanging is not admitted to the Pulag because he has bad karma, other nefarious individuals are banned as well, Perhaps this is why they walk through the woods doing harm. They have no belief in hell. One story says a courageous man that died, went to Pulag, but there he did not want to stay despite the many persuasions of the deceased; he quarreled with them and was returned to earth. From him they knew the existence of this place and furthermore, because many attend in dreams to the requests of the recently dead of this mysterious region. Many dream of going there with the relatives of the deceased, with the sacrificed animals, their furniture and clothes.

Anitos, according to them, are the souls of certain deceased beings that can cause illness and other damage to the living. They are demons; not gods, but evil beings whom they make sacrifices too so they stop hurting, this is important, because anyone would doubt that the Itneg's do not think the same as the Igorot's; but although neighbors, they are mortal enemies of one another. Therefore, it is not surprising that the Anito (singular) is God among the Itnegs, while among the Igorot's, anitos (plural) are devils. Anito is a strange word for the Igorot's and means souls of enemy or foreign men; but the Igorot's also venerate as their guardian angels the souls of their ancestors, whom they call ateng's. Ateng is a ghost, or soul of the deceased.

Christening: when a child is born, one immediately puts water in one's mouth and sprinkles the newborn with it saying: Imitate the water that cleanses everything. Parents of the child are those who later give him a name, changing it whenever he gets seriously ill.

Judgement: A suspected thief or other types of criminals, say Kabunían is the powerful one, and if what is imputed to me is true, I die now; and if not, than I do not die and if there are two suspects, one sticks a pin in the head of both, taking care to introduce the same measure and he who sheds blood first is considered a thief. Which is perhaps explained best by the fact the real culprit's blood rushes to his head from natural fear.

The priest or priestess is called a mambunong. They are praised as the holy sages, and proof of this is that they are all great and revered figures in thier communities, the Igorot's have no idols. the sculptures that sell, they are not such, but only figures of great men and women who sell as objects of curiosity or home decorations. They call little gold idols anitos like the one in our photo engraving, made by Ilocano silversmiths. Around their houses, in the air, you can see an ornate table, made of cane, a meter and a half high, and a meter wide, long by eighty centimeters. It is his altar, it is called bangkilay; there the pig is split, and they put the dishes that are offered to saints and grandparents Deceased.

Kabunían is not offered food, He doesn't need the food of man. In Loó there is another sacred site, as they say that there appeared a saint or some deceased being who asked for sacrifices or offerings. His name was Lumaoig, Lumawíd or Dumaguíd he was a famous man and he married a holy woman of the land, named Dugay or dewhat they had a son, Timlugan. He then announced that he was going to heaven with his son. The people objected to rioting and begged him to even leave his son. He then divided this into two halves. He took one to heaven and there he turned it into Baduang, a man who became famous. After two days, Lumaoig returned to earth to see what the men of the other half had made and found it rotten. He then took her to heaven and turned her into Kirú, the lightning, fire pig; and before thundering, they usually see a pig that climbs the tree, which then appears scorched by lightning. In Benguet, the most famous saint or shaman invoked by the mambunong is Masiken; He follows in importance to his father-in-law Kabígat, whose name means arity, since he is a native of the region from which the sun rises, without being the sun.

There was an old woman named Dugay, who had been very ill for many years, and she instructed her son Timbugan to go and consult the famous shaman Kabígat about her illness. They told him to go where the sun rises and when you see one house, ask where he dwells. He did so and was told to keep going towards the sun and seeing a house with a baliti tree on the roof (this tree only grows in the top of the rocks), to stop in front of it and Kabígat would appear. Indeed this took place and once he arrived, a most beautiful man appeared, it was Kabígat, who learning of his purpose followed him to go and cure his sick mother. Along the way he felt hungry and thirsty; Kabígat told him not to worry about it, and sure enough, when they get to Mount Apunan Kabigat threw a spear at a rock and from it crystal clear water sprouted with many Painted fish which fed them well. Once they reached the home of Dugay, Kabigat made the kañaw called saóúsab, sacrificing a pig and a hen and immediately the sick one was healed.

Dügay is the patron saint of sowing the seed and before harvest preparations they dedicate some offerings to her through the mambunong Ceremony. The mystic 6 masters of the mambunong leave their bodies when they make revelations to them, but in the form of men laughing and joking, they teach them what they ask. In cases of illness, the mambunong puts tafey wine in a tabo (coconut shell) and invokes the diety over the anito and then covers it tightly and places it in a corner. After a quarter of an hour, he uncovers it and reads in it whether it is curable or not, until the Agbúyon suspend a buyo nut (bunga in Tagalog) with a little string and invoke their ancestors (which is what kaísing means), Masíken and Kabígat, who had been commissioned by them to find out by this procedure whatever they wish to know. They ask many questions, and when the nut moves, they understand that it answers affirmatively. This is how they find out if the disease is or is not curable and the kind of animal that should be sacrificed.

The festivities of the Igorot's are: Sabéng, a wedding party where a pig is sacrificed and then another three. Children and parents make marriage contracts and when they are twelve or thirteen years old, they unite them by celebrating that festival. Kapé, party to inaugurate a newly built house; a pig is killed. Pichit or Ságat, according to the dialects of each rancheria, is a great party, bigger than that of the civilized Filipinos, they say. The rich give it by inviting all the fathers, friends and relatives, poor and rich alike, from neighboring towns. Many pigs were killed, dividing one for each neighborhood, and even two, if the neighborhood is large. Pigs, cows and carabao are distributed among neighboring villages and money as well for other animals, the meat of which is to be distributed among the inhabitants of each village. It is solemnized with declamations in verse (dattok), not only the mambunong, but even the elders attending the ceremonies, two days is usually alloted for the celebration of

Pichit and there are thirteen days when pigs are killed during this month. 1st day: Prayer and sacrificing ten pigs. On the 2nd day a cow or a carabao is killed by eating the meat raw with papait. They give meat to those who contribute gifts (solpon). Day 3. A pig is sacrificed that the rich attendees consume, and a pig is also slaughtered for the residents of the rancheria on days 5, 8, 11, 13, 15, 16, 18 and 21. And nothing is done on days 4, 6, 7, 9, 10 and 12 (this day is to be kept between them). On the 13th, a pig is sacrificed with prayers, a cow and a horse, whose meat is distributed among the people of the town as a party for the not very rich. this marks the last day of Pichit. Then many pots or small jars filled with the wine they call tafey, wine made from fermented rice, are received.

Batbat, is a little party to cure diseases. Silk when ordered by the mambunong who does the buyon or ceremony to find out the cause of the disease. They kill a pig and there's dancing in two days. The Segpang or Chawak, according to the rancherias, is like the Batbat. Pigs are sacrificed and there is dancing. *Amdag or Osil* is a little party that is held so that they do not get sick when they dream that they have been injured or something similar. When they forget to do it and get sick, then they do the Aspol ceremony that serves to find out what appeared in dreams: they pray over the jar of tafey and looking at it, they read in it the oracle they want to know then they sacrifice a piglet or a rooster. There is no dancing and entry into the house is prohibited for two days, except those who have attended the party. This prohibition is called Pidiew. He who parties can't get away for two days and snuggles up with his family at his house.

Palís is a party to cure a poisoned person. They sacrifice a dog, a delicacy for them, in the baglan style, that is, dancing with little drums at the door of the dog's house with a machete and spear. The mambunong says that these weapons hurt the poisoner. The musical instruments utilized are five, the guimbal, a large drum with a hole in one end; the sulíbaw, another smaller drum; the goose looks like a basin of metal; the pinsak, small goose; and the palas, another piece of iron. The drums are heated over a fire, so that their skins are stretched, and they are thus refined with the goose and the pinsak. Then they begin to play and dance in front of the party house. They have no more sonat, than one.

Their songs remind me of those of the Japanese. A woman called manárong or manachong dances surrounded by four men: the manáyaw who leads the dance, he carries two blankets on his shoulders; he follows the mangalsa played by the goose; then the maminsak and the mamadas, which leads the palas. In front of the dancers are placed those who play the gimbal and the sulibaw, called respectively mangimbal and mangdibaw. After a few turns, the mambunong intervenes and stops the manayaw, who represents the soul of the celebrated deceased, and then everyone stops and the mambunong screams; I call your attention, ancestors: now that your commemorations have been celebrated, return to your homes until the end of ten years. While the mambunong is speaking, the attendees sing with a single accent: Oway, oway, and then all the attendees shout as far as his lungs reach. Blessings and prayers: They are called ipaltik. first: Attention, brothers and sisters: I hope you're rich and so am I, I hope you all live to have gray hair and so do I. Before drinking the tafey wine, they pray that it does not give them a pain in the stomach, and they say: You old grandparents, old souls who have the tafey, make our work prosper so that we can buy karabaos, pigs and other animals. Another: Oh, Kabunían, who has given the rice that we have made lubud (ground rice that serves as yeast to ferment wine) and tafey, that make us lucky, as well as our work prosperous, so that we may be rich.

The party dancing usually begins with the spouse pronouncing: May you be rich and may all your cows, karabaos, pigs and other properties that you own live, so that there will be another party. It is striking that they do not include the relatives of the celebrated person in the blessing. The person or individuals of the family who pay for these festivities are distinguished by having on their face a bloodstain from the first animal sacrificed. During the festivities many legends are passed down one of which is as follows:

The Igorot's of Sagada (part of Bontok) have provided a legend about the Great Flood, In the beginning the "mother" earth was flat; but one day Kabunían closed the hole where the waters escape and the earth was filled with the liquid element, and all man perished, except two: a man and a woman, who were saved respectively on the summits of the mountains Pagad (to the North) and Kalawitan (South). The woman lit a fire by rubbing some reeds, and when the man saw the smoke, she mounted a guimbal (drum, in the shape of a cube one and a half meters long by thirty centimeters wide) and went to the other summit. He helped the woman to produce fire and they sat there for a month contemplating the flood that drowned everything, because Kabunían had gone down to them on the mountain top and ordered them not to fornicate until a month passed, they obeyed and it was then that the waters receded and they saw for the first time that there were mountains, abysses, rivers, sea's and other unevenness upon the earth, then Kabunian returned descending down to them and instructed them to marry and procreate for the purpose of renewing the human race, Kabunian then gave them the rice plant and other seeds, so that they would have food and agriculture . These first people were called Adan and Iban; they had eight children who married to each other, and engendered the human race. "Ah, that's Adam and Eve, and the antediluvian patriarchs" some outsiders interrupted, but the elder replied: "No, It will be you who have imitated our legends".

They also told me the following legend, which is similar to

accounts about the apparitions of Buddha. "One day Kabunían appeared in Bontok in the form of an ugly man full of sores and married a virtuous woman (Bángan). Her brothers and her sisters, made fun of her husband's ugliness; but she always answered them like this: that since he was her husband, she loved him in spite of everything and on a kañaw day they all went to the mountain with spears, armor and salakots (helmets) and as they became thirsty and the rumor was already spreading that the oldman was Kabunían, his younger brother-in-law, in a mockery, told him "Since you're getting the word out that you're Kabunían, why don't you make a fountain sprout and let's drink?" Then the old man threw a spear at a rock and water gushed out, it was then he said: Now, everyone can drink but you will be the last (to the brother-in-law). The people drank and finally the brother-in-law approached quenching his thirst, and while he was drinking, Kabunían slapped him, and he remained glued to the fountain. Until now, a rock in the form of a man has been pointed out in Bontok, the spring of Kabunian still gushes from it today".

The elder continued: "Kabunían planted a plantation of abas (tubers) here, and these abas, if they are cut by the root, the next morning They reappear as if they had not been cut. He had three children by his wife and one day he told her: those from above (heaven) do not allow me to remain married to a woman of the earth, so I'll have to return and we'll share the children. They did so, dividing the third into two halves and Kabunían took to heaven his part which was Lumaoig. Kabunían's wife contemplated emotionally on what the other half that corresponded with her woul be and at that moment her half became a real girl".

It seems that this couple is the one that gave rise to the human race, perhaps Kabígat and Búgan. According to those of Benguet, Kabígat was the first man who existed in the world, the wisest and most powerful; but not God. As we have seen, it was the woman from Dumaguid who went to consult him. They don't know the name of Kabígat's wife. They ignore what the word Igorot or igodót means and say that it is Ilocano, with whose denomination the Ilocanos distinguish them, implying that they are not Christians.

CHAPTER 12
CULT OF THE ITNEGS

These who walk a thin line between nomadic hunter-gatherers and the "civilized world" the intermediates between the tribal Igorot's and the civilized Filipinos; the intnegs are clothed while the Igorot only wears a loincloth, they claim to be monotheists, as were the civilized Filipino's upon the arrival of the first Spaniard's. It is necessary to investigate further the beliefs, legends and superstitions of the Itneg's, since it seems to me beyond doubt that among them the ancient religion of the civilized Filipinos is still preserved.

The Itnegs worship an Anito God, creator of everything, omnipotent, wise, good and just that punishes the wicked. Their images consist of crude stone idols, as has been said. When one dies, they say: Inamet ta Anito (Anito took him), and they believe that he goes to the mountains and spends time there singing, paradise, then for them is located on a mountain like the ancient Filipinos, Hindus, Persians, Hebrews and Greeks. They have three kinds of little houses dedicated to the Anito, and it is strange that no idols are found in them. These are found in uninhabited places in the open or in the shade of some tree of venerable appearance for its foliage. Each dwelling is surrounded by a tiny cane house one meter high and front by half a meter deep, one-story high with a kogon roof and one room,(that is, there is a main floor or mezzanine), without walls. In these little houses, the old women offer food to the Anito in cases of illness or other matters of importance.

Murmuring prayers the worshipper puts eight or seven

pipes in a row, whose ends are cut staggered so that the liquid slides as on a ladder. When these little houses are repaired, other festivals are given, without which the smallest piece of cane or kogon cannot be touched or removed. Thus, they leave them to the destructive sands of time, or if the owner lacks resources for parties of repair. The Anito's priests both men and women, are called baglans, which must have been their real name, and not babaylan or katalonan. The priest's consecrate the stones intended to be idols and give names to newborns, hitting the trunk of a tree with a machete, and when they want to find out the fate of a sick person, the baglan unloads a blow with the aliwa (very sharp axe) on a part of the heart of a piglet and immediately puts his hand to the wound, to see if the heart has come out of it, in which case the patient will be relieved, and if not, he is disillusioned, which reminds us of the red haruspices who also read in the bones of the victims what they wanted to know.

Shamanism: When you go to the oracle of a priestess, she prepares a rooster of those born destined for sacrifice, which are those with white feathers with legs of yellow scales, as those are considered Anito's property, they are not to be sold, given away, or eaten. The Itneg Pythoness (high priestess) begins her rites by chanting, begging the Anito to reveal what she wants to know; while she is speaking, she walks around the house, raising her voice more and more, and continuing like this, she picks up the Anito's rooster or hen and goes out onto the roof or part of the uncovered house and makes some signs with the rooster in her hand, as if to call the Anito; Finally, she cuts the victim's throat and runs to join the patient with the freshly sacrificed blood.

She returns to the roof continuously talking, and when the wind blows, on whose wings the Itnegs believe that the Anito arrives, it flies into the baglan at the sickbed, at this moment she faints and convulses at this moment the Anito has already entered the host. Anyone would suppose that they cunningly take advantage of the first gust of wind that comes; but they assure that when the anito comes on the wings of a strong wind, it only blows where the baglan is in convulsions, the leaves of the nearby trees remaining motionless. According to Williams, the same thing happens in the Fiji Islands and the possessed exclaims: Koi au, koi auí (It's me, it's me!) as, according to the Exodus, God exclaimed when appearing to Moses: I am. And when the spirit leaves him, the enlightened man falls violently to the ground, like the Philippine baglan.

One of the house members then approaches to ask her if the disease is curable or not, and the Anito answers through her mouth, the questions asked, the Sibyl regains her senses, and then gets dressed and they eat the rooster. In Ilocos and in the other Philippine provinces, remains of similar sibyltic practices are still preserved. There, days after a death has occurred, or without occurring, some woman feels attacked from the inside out. shaking or convulsing, they cover her with a black cloak (lambong in tagalog), and they ask her questions, believing that the soul of the recently deceased possessed her, and she is the one who answers with her own voice.

Fray Gaspar de San Agustin (1698) said: It seems that these practices were introduced among the Bisaya's a few years before the coming of Magellan and that they originated from the Gentiles of the East, although they are not known from which kingdom particularly, or if possibly from China, where they are very numerous and are called Tiao Kei, which refers to the ceremonies similar to those of the Itnegs that the Visayams also practiced, Legazpi referred to them in his memorial to the King of Spain even before arriving in Manila. It is what Sir John Lubbock calls Shamanism, and it is common in Siberia, the Philippines and other parts of East Asia. We believe in many instances it is about special people, usually women, and as the effects become stranger and more incomprehensible, to the outside world, it can begin to be attributed to some deceased child or soul that gets into the group of the living, to carry out some errand.

Among those present there is no lack of someone who lends themself to interpreting the message by relating it to some pending family issue, many times in good faith, and others, proposing a favorable solution to the interests they may wish to protect.

Mystics and Shamans in the Philippines in general are also closely related to the mystery and power of dreams. One of the famous researchers on the topic Burton in Abeo Kuta, regarding the indigenous people of Yoruba (West Africa) believe that dreams are revelations of the dead; or revelations of the good gods, according to those tribes of Madagascar (The Adventures of Robert Drury). The ancient Herodotus had said that when the Nasamones wished to divine, they went to the tombs of their ancestors.

Shamanism is one of the manifestations of Anitería or worship of the spirits of the ancestors. Not directly from a Filipino source, but by some foreign authors we are informed that the Itnegs speak of Gods, one of which is very similar to the ancient Pan, some believe these legends to be variations of the mythos regarding Dasiasoias and Iuananguan who travels through space and time on horseback killing abandoned children. Among the Mountain tribes of Abra there is a superstitious period of the year called kañaw, in which they need to cut the throat of some man, and they go out to lie in wait for the neighboring tribes and cut the throat of the most careless or arrogant one, who is usually a boy, girl, or old person. Right now, when people in the Philippines try to scare children, they are threatened that a bandit is coming, whose misdeeds are feared. We believe, then, that this Iuananguan, like Nagbuyagan, were at first one of those Igorot's who lie in wait to kill the careless. All the fantastical beings that kill abandoned children must have come from an origin such as this.

CHAPTER 13

RESURRECTION OF SANKABAGWAY

Next comes the neighboring province of Ilocos and the tribes of the Itnegs, Igorot's, and the Aeta; among Filipinos, they are the ones who should keep the old Philippine Religion less adulterated because they are further north, and although the Mohammedan's from the South also arrived there from Mindanao, Joló, or Paragua usually, it was only to loot their coastal settlements. Even in my lifetime those memories remain when those Malay Moor pirates came to Ilocos, and the stories were handed down to me by my Grandparents.

The Ilocanos believed in the existence of a Creator, as evidenced by the fact that they have the word Namarsuá, with which they designate to God and means creator, but in reality he was nothing more than a gigantic builder, because according to the council, he did not get to be something from nothing, but everything was done with the already existing raw materials. It corresponds to the Maykapal (the Maker), supreme God of the Tagalogs. The study of this great Architect constitutes a true discovery and will fix the ancient concept that the Filipinos had of God that until now has been mistakenly believed to be the tigmanukín bird, when it was not even called that, but tigmamanok.

Let's analyze that Supreme Maker motif was it a deified man (Anito), a spiritual being, star, or bird. It was an erroneous interpretation of what Father Carro had said in the Ilocano Dictionary, the affirmation that Boni was the God of the Ilocanos, since the aforementioned author did not refer to us as the Ilocanos, but as the infidels, and those who had this name when he wrote this were the Igorot's. Buni or Kabunían, in fact, is the god of the Igorot's of the Kiangan. Contemporary Ilocanos say: that in the beginning there was a man called Angngaló, so tall that standing on the earth, he touched his head on the celestial vault and with one step he went from Vígan to Manila, a distance of sixty-one leagues.

As the ancient Filipinos made their bamboo houses, raising the roof already formed, they say that Angngaló raised and placed the celestial roof, as well as its lamps: the sun, the moon and the stars. He dug the ground that was previously flat and the lands that he extracted are today the mountains, the hills being the portions that escaped from the interstices of his poorly joined fingers. He then made an abyss and he relieved the bladder of it and formed the seas and rivers. His waters at first were not salty, but those of the sea became salty as a result of the fact that on the occasion that he was taking his three daughters to Manila to sell salt, by accident they fell into it with his loads. We have no doubt that Agngaló must be the King of Creation that they only vaguely remember today.

The distinguished Tagalog writer Mariano Ponce speaks in his Folklore Bulakeño, and the same one who would gird the rainbow like a loincloth or sash, for which it is called bahag-hari, or king's loincloth giving to understand that he was naked like the Igorot's or the Aeta; and the one who wove such immense straw would be his wife Aran, the Dauani of the Bicolano's. The thunder would come to be her voice, as the Indigenous tribes of other countries believe. The giants of the Tagalogs: from Síbul (Bulacan) I have collected the following legend: At first the sky was very low and because of the heat it was not possible to live on earth. Then came a giant so tall that he stooped under the vault of heaven and lifted it up. And since the heat of the sun's eyes was still unbearable, with an owl (cane-bojo) he pierced one of his eyes. Since then, the sun is one-eyed and its heat bearable. The footprints of this giant are preserved near Sibul, in San Mateo and in the

Norzagaray River. At this last point he is up to the tracks of his dog. They call this giant Cristóbal, confusing him with the legendary giant of Catholicism; but his true name must have been Meykapal, that is, the one who formed the world.

Angngaló and Aran at first would be simple legendary ancestors, like the Sukuk and Mingan of the Kapampangan's; but later it seems that they were formed myths that have meaning. On one of the mountains beyond the mouth of the Abra River, to the right, coming from Ilocos Sur, I saw a cleft in the earth about a hundred meters long that from afar looks like a human footprint. They say that it is from Angngaló and that there is another on Mount Bulagaw, which must have been the Paradise of those of that region. Tagalog elders have told me that there are similar traces in the mountains of Mariveles and San Mateo and that they attribute it to the King of creation which confirms that he and Angngaló were the same person.

One of the great subterranean cave systems of Abra is indicated as the matrix of Aran, and from here I deduce that in the mythical interpretation, Aran is the Earth and that Angngaló is the Supreme Maker of immeasurable power, that is God. The Igorot's call the Earth mother. At the bottom of the myth of Angngaló and Aran we see nothing but the ancient myth that beings were born from the copulation between Heaven and Earth.

The Egyptians said that Khum or Shem, their Hercules (the Hara Kala of India) who defeated the giants, impregnated the goddess Sati or Anuke, are symbols of matter. The Greeks sang that the Sky (Uranus) fertilized the Earth (Ghe or Gea) and engendered the Centimanos, the Cyclops, and or the Titans. According to the Phoenicians, Kolp (the sky or luminous space) fertilized the Earth (Achera) or the primordial slime (Bahu). Two Malays, brothers of the Filipinos, believe they have been fathered by Heaven and Earth. So, believe some tribes of alfuros of Ceram, adding that tremors are produced by the efforts of the earth to restore its former state, and so do other Malays. The Javanese call heaven(Koso) father (Bopo) and earth (Pratiswi) mother (Ibu). Brahma, the creator of the Hindus, was also a giant at the time of creation. Angngaló must be the Philippine Atlas that the outside chroniclers B.B. vaguely heard about.

Buceta y Bravo, Historical Geographical Dictionary of the Philippines 1850; made up for the lack of exact news about it with those invented by Colin by amplifying those of Quirino. We have not been able to verify this new cosmogony neither among the Filipinos nor in other authors older than them, and I think I have discovered the sources of their data.

They attributed to the Filipinos the legend that "supported the earth by a giant, he made a movement forced by fatigue, and the earth was submerged in the seas, leaving only scattered islands to men. This is the Atlas, in mythology, supported the world on its waters, and whose swelling changed the ancient form of the earth". My objection: The ancient Filipinos, due to their scarce means of communication and the insurmountable difficulties that were offered to the same They ignored that our Archipelago was made up of small islands, and they believed that the earth was a continent that could be traveled to where the dome of heaven begins and rises. To get there, our grandparents used to say, you always need to walk from when you are born until you are old.

A note regarding the two Babylon's, we read that Ivan and Kallery attributes to Japan a mythology similar to Atlas. We have not read that mythology and we cannot say if it is closer to our Angngaló, or if they copied Buceta and Bravo. In China, near Fochow, above the Mingan ports, there is also a traditional imprint called Mandarin's Boot. In Ceylon, on the top of Adam's Peak, there is another giant footprint attributed to Adam. Some peoples, like the Slavs and Germans, say that Adam and Eve were giants; but the Hindus attribute this imprint to Buddha and say that it was imprinted with the force with which he jumped into the sky. Others attribute it to the muddy state of the land at the beginning, which is less implausible. So, regarding the legend of Aran and Angnalo, I find the legend accurate.

Quirino transmitted that the first man came out of a reed bush and until now, when one jokingly says that he was not born of a woman, the Ilocano's reply: "Then you were born from a reed". In the reedbeds of the Philippines, fish called buan-buan usually grow inside the reeds, in their bush. In Ilocano buan-buan, In tagalog and in Spanish it means fish of the moon or lunar. This seems to them like a phenomenon of nature, because they do not see the the hole where said fish has slipped away. In an analogous way they will have assumed that the first men must have been born from a reed (3). Remember that when Angngaló formed the sky, the mountains and the seas, the flat earth already existed, and therefore, reeds and other plants could have existed before the first men and animals. In cosmogonies, plants usually appear before animals. animals, because without them they would not eat. It follows from this that the creation of the first beings was spontaneous.

Thus, indeed do the Indigenous tribes believe that in the beginning everything arose from the earth spontaneously as now the plants sprout from it. The three daughters of Angnaló, whose names we do not know, resemble the saints of the Igorot's. Bángan, Dúgay and Búgan, mothers of the human race or to the three daughters of the enchanted Sukú of the pampangans, which seem may be the same. It appears that they represent the gods or inventors of Salt, Rice and Gold. The Ilocanos give the divine treatment of Apo (Lord) to these indispensable things and there is a Goddess called Balitok (gold). The rice that is her bread would symbolize the food, salt the vegetables, and since the ancient Filipinos lacked money, the gold would represent riches. The Bagobos of Mindanao speak of a giant Tagamaling and Damakolen who formed the mountains. The name of Angngaló recalls the anito Mángalo of the Visayas and Mangalok of the Bulalakaweño's of Paragua(Palawan). If among them, those were bad entities, it must have been because of hatred of race or religion between the different regions of the Archipelago. On the other hand, for the Tingguianes, Manalok, which must be the same Mangalok, is the most respected of the diuatas. We believe that the Supreme God of the Ilocanos, and probably of all the other civilized Filipinos, was Angngaló, because all the creators were the supreme god of the many Filipino peoples; and his main attribute was that of Creator (Namarsuá or Lumaláng), Maker (Maykapal).

In the religious system of the amazulús, from Rev. Callaway, in his antithesis, we find Unkulonkulo, their Adam or father of their tribes. He is somewhat similar to Angngaló because of his name, because he was born from a cane field and because he is not an object of worship, and according to Rev. Merolla, those of West Africa say that those who made the world were our ancestors, supposing it impossible that the earth and the sky were the work of an invisible and incorporeal Being, The same is believed by the Basutos. According to Casalis, Angngaló like Kabunían and other supreme gods of our diverse mountain tribes, he must have been some deified ancestor, due to his wisdom or ingenuity, (this was affirmed by an enlightened Igorot), this was in the remote times, when even the Filipinos of the coasts did not wear dresses. Now the Ilocanos no longer remember that Angngaló was adored, but they still have retained the oral tradition, that he worked heaven and earth by the order of God; moreover, this new hybrid legend must have been a mystification of Christianity that, nearly four centuries ago, they embraced in such a way that it even horrifies them now as a great heresy or ridiculous nonsense when it comes to their ancient Religion.

The Roman priests having succeeded in making them believe that their ancient Gods were the demons, which is an unspeakable deception, because if within the Romanist dogma there are anitos or saints protectors, it will always be more logical to invoke the souls of ancestors than those of strangers who we do not know. If they were true saints, because, according to their history, the main ones were the friars, who like the ones we all saw here with our own eyes, had many innocent Christians killed, accusing them of being Masons or freebooters, and others erased from history as if they have not even existed like the three wise men Gaspar, Melchor, and Baltazar. Because this Boudica interpolation is false. St. Matthew does not say that they were kings or that they were called that, nor do these names appear in the royal chronologies of Persia, Assyria or Damascus. According to Morga, the ancient Filipinos venerated the skulls as if they were alive and had them present in thier daily lives and customs. Our Dr. Rizal comments: "We find it much more pious to venerate the remains of the parents to whom they owe almost everything and call the second gods of the earth, than not to venerate and revere the memory, bones, hair, etc. of certain saints, many of which they were strange maniac's and of such doubtful sanctity, that what Saint Augustine said can be applied to them: "that they are adored where they are not, and where they are, they are burned".

We are all equally children of two, and if our common Father gave Saints to the Europeans, it was just that he should give his to the ancient Filipinos, because it would be absurd for him to have created them all for hell. In the new Catechism published by Pope Pius X it is said that the pagans who keep a holy life, if they die, also go to heaven, even if they are not baptized, because he rightly asserts, that although they are not Christians, in the ritual or external, they are in the fundamental, which is the worship of God through a virtuous and charitable heart, we add from Angngaló down to the cult of the Ilocanos, whom were Animist's or Anitismist's. They believed that the dead man, his shadow survived, half spiritual, half visible; that same synthesis of organized matter and spirit that according to the principles of spiritism & philosophy, serves to constitute the animal being and the human being by means of a fluidic organic and plastic bond, which is called the Peri-spirit, Meta-spirit or aerial body. It is like a gaseous emanation that is formed with the vapors that perspire through the pores of the body. In the other life it is almost the same as before; but it is already semi-spiritual; it is sustained by our food, but only with its substance.

Thus, they leave the offered dishes visibly intact, but already bland and unusable. The spirits or shadows commonly live in the woods, uninhabited places, in the weeds or orchards of the towns and in empty houses. When the living pass through these places, they usually lose their spirit, because it entertains itself with them and stays. Then the loser falls as alienated without shadow or reason, so that spirit is the same reason; It differs from the soul, as we understand it now, in that the latter is incorporeal, and the former has an aerial body that is visible like a shadow, and sometimes it is palpable.

The spirits of the dead can enter the body of the living to carry out errands or to annoy, and so do the Malays believe the same. All who die, from fetuses to the elderly, leave behind a spirit that survives them. The spirits of the fetuses, envious of our life, which they have not been able to enjoy, sometimes mislead the living, except for their relatives and friends of the family. Tagalog's say they are called Patiának, Pati in Sanskrit means Lord, and Anak means son. Patianak, it is therefore, Lord son, or son of the Anito. In southern Ilocos, the Anito they are called kibaan or kaibaan, and in northern Ilocos, Sankabagway. The imagination of ancient man was as playful and fanciful as that of children, and what he did not know, he supplied, and even enlarged, with the chimeras he imagined. The nocturnal songs of the cricket and the like, and the lights of the fireflies, he attributed to these spirits; as they nest in the trees and undergrowth, he supposed that these were the abodes of said spirits, believing that the songs of the orthoptera are the strums of the Kibaan's tiny guitar, and the fireflies are his lamps. Fireflies, they are called in Bicol aninipot, from the same root ani, soul. The howl of some dog or the meow of a lost cat was taken as the cry of the Patianak, and from a mere supposition they immediately went on to affirm that they had seen the Patianak in the form of a newborn child.

A fifteen-year-old village girl became famous in Vigan in 1876, because the people believed she had many kaiban's inside her body, she told us that one afternoon she was surprised to see tiny children on a fence that were no taller than a foot, and she was delighted, so she picked them up on her apron; Then they disappeared, going into her body, they became her friend's and made her an oracle. She sat in the open-air half a yard away from us, a few spectators were around, An aunt of hers began to call the spirits by their names, to those of the Christians like Ciriaco etc. and without taking off the lips of her the girl, she answered her as a slight whistle that seemed to come out of her, possibly out of her nose; moreover, she was completely still and without taking any deep breaths. So, this went on for a good amount of time and no one could understand it; but the interpreter dismissed herself to her liking, saying that the other spirits were sleeping until the awakened one also went to sleep.

According to this, the Kibaan's sleep, they get scalded if we pour boiling water on them, and they still die. They are not demons or evil; they are simply like us, good with the good, and bad with the bad. These are some of thier attributes: their friends they give them a lot of gold, a cape that makes them invisible, a bowl of coconut shell that gives inexhaustible rice, a small pot of clay that offers delicacies of all kinds, and talismans that satisfy whatever they need and desire. To those who spill hot water, without warning. They throw some powder at them that causes annoying skin diseases. When they appear to men, they open their mouths, from which comes a dazzling light, which undoubtedly is some will-o'-the-wisp they have seen. They are of two sexes and procreate with men and women, like demons, incubi and succubus of the Romanists, of whom perhaps This detail was imitated.

When a Kibaan married to a human woman dies, if she honors her widowhood, the surviving Kibaan's give her the goods left by the deceased. The other Philippine peoples also speak of dwarf anitos (kukú or pandak), and they must be the same souls of the fetuses and those of the dead children. There are Kibaan's who are the height of a one-year-old child.

The Lítaw, male genus of the water, he looks like a drowned siren girl. Let us remember that the souls of the drowned, according to the ancients, remained in the water. They designate another river goddess, who, according to legend was a girl who attracted by the clarity of a stream went down to pick up a lost needle and was caught and charmed by Lítaw. This type of goddess is now called a Mermaid; her legend was adulterated with fantastic details taken from or similar to fairy tales found in the Thousand and One Nights; but formerly she would be the Sinaya or Amansinaya, goddess of the water of the old Tagalog's, which would not be more than the soul of a drowned girl that turned into an anito of the liquid element.

The Ilocanos speak of a black giant that lives in uninhabited houses, it is called Pugot (black). It is easy to guess that he must be the soul of an aeta, one of those who are buried in their houses, which are later abandoned. They have tree rings, to whom they ask permission to penetrate forests or cut down trees. They are called mangmangkik and would be the souls of those who were buried there. The katatawan are fabulous beings that cross space on airships. Surely, those are the souls of the fishermen or sailors who were buried in their own boats so that they could continue the same way of life that they had before. It must come from the root taaw, sea, that is, an anito de mar, or anito of the ocean. Katao in Bisaya is, in effect, a sea monster in a human figure with a half-body on top and repeats what it hears.

In Bangi (Northern llocos) at the site of Lákay-lákay, when turning in the direction of Aparri, there are two rocks that at ten fathoms are so similar to an old woman and to an ancient salakot, that They make me suspect that an ancient "great civilization" as Reclus of Oceania in general states, As the navigators pass by, they offer them some of their cargo. Otherwise, they believe that the wind or the tide would not let them pass. The Ilocanos suppose that the souls of the wicked sometimes incarnate in animals. Forty years ago, they reported that the soul of a certain Lorenzo Manangkong incarnated in a consumptive dog that walked the streets of Vígan, to atone for his sins as a usurper.

The Ilocanos are very sure that their deceased fathers, mothers and children continue to love them and take an interest in them; they still usually visit them, especially on the third and ninth day after their death, for which they always keep the windows of the mortuary house open and dust the entrances with ashes or sand so that their footprints are known. Grandparents, due to the greater veneration they inspired in them, were considered demigods or true Anitos. If that ancestor had been famous for his wisdom, for his exploits or for his successes, with time and legend his figure would become more gigantic until he became a true God, and if his devotees had come to know Astronomy, they would make him an astronomical God, and, progressing further, a purely spiritual one.

Did the Ilocanos have demons in the sense of tempters? they had good and protective Anitos that were the souls of the ancestors; and those who were bad in life, or were personal or tribal enemies, continued to be bad or evil, causing harm, they became their demons, which they called dákes (bad) ósairo (perverse), like the asura, Sanskrit, which means the same.

One of those bad Anitos is the soul of an old Itneg woman, who in times of smallpox appears offering corn to children, and if they take it, they contract said disease, this will have originated from the fame of poisoners that the Itnegs have. There is another old woman who inspires the maibangoángon (visionaries). The curious thing is that the Ilocanos, like the Tribes from the North, do not know the Aswang or anything similar.

They had witches and goblins, but kept their Castilian names, which reveal their origin. The friars and Jesuits brought us their superstitions. If you come to Spain, you would be surprised that almost all our fables and superstitions are identical there. The Aswang must be an imported superstition. Zoanthropy or the mania of believing oneself to have become a sorcerer or an animal was in vogue in Europe at the time the Spaniards first arrived in the Philippines. These witches seem exotic among those from the North of Luzon, although the literature about them is incomplete and similar in part to the Spanish councils, and in part to the Malaysians.

According to the Ilocanos, the owl is like the dog that accompanies the witch. She walks through the space with half her body from the waist up, announcing herself with her high-pitched and terrifying song. She hurts whoever she finds. The salaksaky blue bird is the size of the thrush, although smaller, is similar to the batala bird of the Kapampangan's, which is the same tigmamanok of the Tagalogs according to others. It is a bird of omen for the

Ilocanos, they speak of Kúmaw a fabulous bird of great proportions that catches abandoned children and probably at first, it was nothing more than some sacred item or food offering that he stole from unwary children, like the Iwananguan of the Itnegs.

The Tagalogs, they tell us about the Adama bird, whose excrement turns men into stone; but it seems to be of an exotic origin. They mention a prodigious light coming out of the mouth of the extraordinary roosters which can cast a powerful amulet. They call it mutiá like the Tagalogs. They would believe that this mutiá is the soul of the rooster, because according to the ancient races, all beings and even objects that have a shadow are endowed with a soul. The beginning of their belief would be some will-o'-the-wisp that they will have, seen to appear casually near the mouth of a rooster.

To the Sun and the Moon they also give the divine title of Apo (Lord), and they narrate that the spots of the last one are a tree and a man asleep in its shadow; it is Saint Joseph when he abandoned Mary in despair, so they say now; but formerly he would be another man, probably the man the Igorot's think they see riding on the moon, when a man dies; or perhaps the old woman who, according to the Iroquois, is there eternally spinning, perhaps the weaver Dawani of the Bicolano's, or Aran. This would agree with what Villaverde stated that the stars are the abodes of the deities of the mountains of Luzon. According to today's Ilocanos, lightning begins as a white pig or rooster that later turns into fire, and thunder is its growl. This obviously is a corruption of an ancient belief. The white pig and chicken are the ones chosen for Anito sacrifices. The neighboring Igorot's say that when he thunders, Kirul asks for a pig or chicken. Therefore, the ancient belief would be that when it thunders, the Anito eats some white pig or chicken. The Ilocanos had, in addition to the aforementioned visionaries, diviners, summoners, which the Tagalogs call manghuhula, pitho or pithi, the mannílaw that look for stolen or missing objects with lights.

CHAPTER 14

RELIGION OF THE CAGAYANOS

The ancient's entertained the same beliefs as the Ilocano's and Mountain Tribe's, their neighbors, that is the cult of the Anitos with their priestesses. For adoration houses they had some huts like those described for the Itnegs, and images of their Anitos, who sometimes dreamed of seeing reincarnated as karabaos, as black men or as little country women (Kibaan's), who attracted the unwary to harm them. Her visionary priestesses asked Anito for gold and jewels, and they dreamed that she would give them many gold bracelets and strings of valuable stones; but when they woke up, they evaporated (Aduarte, p. 141 -143); and this was surely what the credulous González de Mendoza took for granted. Fray Aduarte writes: (The Kagayans) "sometimes asked their Anito to let himself be seen, and he replied that his body was so beautiful that they couldn't see him; once certain Indians begged him very earnestly to get down from above the house, where I was talking about in (107) Kagayao dialect, and came to talk with them, fell then in the midst of those who were there a stone of much esteem among them, which they call maxin and he was shaking for a good while on the ground and from there he spoke with a small and thin voice and at last the stone and the demon disappeared" (p. 142). It was undoubtedly a dream like the other cases that he himself says that they had dreamed them; but the visionaries would tell them so in good faith that all the friar chroniclers gave them as true. They believed in the resurrection of the dead, according to Aduarte, page, 163; and to this day, the Mountain Tribe's of Isabela de Luzon tell of a marriage that returned from the world of the dead, according to Fray Villaverde.

CHAPTER 15

TEMPLE OF THE KAPAMPANGANS

We have obtained from our studies the evidence that the civilized peoples, that is, those of the coasts, had a single Religion, evident proof that they were not tribes that were exterminated in daily fights, but a great confederated people. There were only slight variants due to the difference in dialects and ancestors of each family; basically, and in the general lines there was only one Religion. Anyone can verify it by digging a little in the comparable Folk-Lore of the various provinces. Only the friars who could not penetrate the interiorities of our beliefs, because they persecuted them, could think otherwise. Many anitos are the same, with different names, while others were not registered in the other towns. These will serve us to complete our general mythology of pangasinan, only Anagaoley is mentioned in the ancient chronicles, to whom they offered oils, ointments and aromatic plants; and if he asked for it, even slaves were sacrificed to him. It's the same Anito supreme of the other Filipinos. His name reminds us to Angngaló. ApoLaki (Lord Laki) was his war anito and he seems general even to the Apayaos of Ilocos Norte, who also adore him. Aglai-Ialaki means heroic in English. The supreme Anito of the Zambales was Malyari, the owner of power, and it seems to mean the same as Meykapal or Mayari (owner/creator of the land?) Ahasi, was the protective anito, whom they invoked in their tribulations and illnesses. Manglabat, anito of peace, placate the godless, like the relatives of someone murdered. Mangalagar, was the savior for those in dangers; they sacrificed to him "when they came out of a war the victors. Aniton tavo the lord of the wind and the rains. Dumangan, to whom they prayed so that the rice grained. Kalasakas, ripens it.

Damulag delivers it in bloom, from hurricanes. It seems that it was a baby that once incarnated in a carabao or buffalo of those that look like venerable sphinxes. His name means this useful animal. The Kapampangan's are the point of union between the previous provinces and the Tagalogs, with whom they have a great similarity of traditions. They also had an Anito called Bátala (without the h), a blue bird with a red beak and a long, white breast tigmamanok in Tagalog. But the ominous one is the kásay-kásay and not the tigmamanok. They professed the cult of the Anitos, which they called Iraya, which means shadow or spectrum; corresponds to the Araría, of the Ilocanos that means the same; and to Anito of the Igorot's. They know the male anito del agua, but with the Castilian name of Sereno or Siúkuy tagalog. Everything that we will say about the Tagalogs can be extended to the Kapampangan's, since they also know the Aswang, the Tikbalang, the Patianak, etc. They call God Linaláng or Makirapát equivalent to Meykapal. His supreme Anito seems to be the venerable old man Sukú, one who was principal in life and now lives in a whitewashed palace on Mount Sinukuan (Aráyat). The Kapampangan's ask him for permission to walk through those forests or take some fruit or tree from them, giving him the treatment of Apo (Lord or Grandparent), otherwise, he strikes them down with lightning. In the Paradise of Sinukuan there is an enchanted bronze palace, which is lost in the heights. Sukú is there on an ebony lankape (sofa) adorned with gold and precious stones. They follow the same traditional way of life as before. The food is served to him by enchantment and then the rays collect and clean up the waste. This palace has seven doors guarded respectively by a lion, a tiger, a bear, a viper, a snake, an ita (negrito) and a sagasa a bird with a curved beak and a fierce appearance. All of which recalls the Hindu legends (see Philippine Bible, p. 32). I understand that in Pampanga or in all of Luzon there is no tiger, lion or bear, which is proof that these enchantments and legends have their origin in Hinduism, Sukú has a black child as a servant who brings him grains of gold as if they were gingers that he pulls from the root of the earth; he has kids that lay down gold; cows that by droppings leave fine tissues. Mingan, the wife of Sukú, settled down in the neighboring mountain. They have three daughters and several sons. Those are like nymphs of beauty and attract unwary young people with their spells, to punish the wicked, and only a judicious, good and brave young man would be worthy of their favors. (See Kapampangan Folk-Lore of Mr. Pedro Serrano Laktaw).

CHAPTER 16

AND GOD SO LOVED
THE TAGALOGS

It is the same Anitería of the previous towns. Maykapal must be the same Namarsuá or Angngaló of the Ilocanos, the one that Mr. Ponce calls "King of Creation" the kibaan is the Patianak or tawong damo; the litaw is the siukuy, the aningaas is the tayabo kakap, and the kalag is the Bisaya and bíkol (semi-material soul).The Bisaya Aswang already appears, a name that the northern provinces do not use, except for the witch (still in Spanish) introduced by the Spaniards, as its name indicates. And instead of the treatment of Apa that the North and South of Luzon give to their children, according to the Spaniards, as her name indicates. They used another word of Sanskrit origin, the badhala or bathala, which means the same; but now they say: Bathalang Maykapal, Bathalang San José; otherwise Panginoong God, Panginoong Saint Joseph, and the Panginoon means "Lord," like Rev. In my humble opinion, the name of their supreme god was Maykapal or Lumikha, and hence that is why they call their sacred images likha, and not Badhala, Because this last word was not a specific name, but for some Tagalogs Anitos carried the title of Lakan or prince, so it seems undoubted that they were Deified leaders, such as Lakan-Datan. Lakan-Pati or Anito de sementera, according to a foreigner he was a hermaphrodite; but we suppose that they would be anitos of different sexes that can have dealings with men and women, as they say of the Kibaan's. We don't know if It was Indianake himself, a farm deity. Lakan-bakod or Lakan-bakor, close guard, must be and the same Kibaan that nests in the plants that serve as fences. They asked him to cure his diseases, such as The Ilocanos to their country years, Lakan-bui or Lakan-busog, or Lakanbini, where to eat, Like Kibaan gives his friends a pot that produces all kinds of meals. It's missing alanito Bisaya Makabosog, how fed up. Bokong or Boking, was another of his children. The family children were called dingali. Amani Kable or Amanikoable, God of the hunters. It is said that they had an idol called Linga. They must have meant likha. We do not believe that it is the Lingam of the Hindus, the organ of generation, Silagan or witch Siligan that destroys the livers of those who wear white; it must be the same as the Aswang. Lahó, the monster that wants to devour the sun or the moon in eclipses, is of Malay origin, if not that the Malays are the ones who took it from the Filipinos. The Javanese and Maguindanao call it rahu (the / and r are confused in Filipino and Malay dialects) or karawn. The Dayaks know of three monsters rahobawang (golden dragon), rahotumbaga (copper dragon) and rahoatnbon (fog dragon) and other Malays naga which is the name given by the Hindus to their fabulous serpent, and according to Blumentritt, the tirurays of Mindaraw also call the fabulous eight-headed fish naga that is supposed to inhabit the navel (center) of the sea; but it is not in the Tiruray Dictionary where he got his data from. In Bíkol Bakunawa is the alligator whose movements produce the tremors And they feared the souls of the enemy tribes as harmful Guardian's, They believed in the reincarnation of the souls of the fetuses in the Pati-Anak (lord son), who appears and cries in the desert like a newborn child, or in a kind of goblin that, like the Kibaan's of the Ilocanos, makes love to women or men, depending on the sex. old Tagalog's, according to Blumentritt, or the Tomar that is par gone to the Patianak? We think that a fetus soul is the Patianak and the older ones who are already capable of falling in love are those of older children. squatting, knees pass head; other times he appears as a horse with human skin and manes like those of a porcupine. Among the spikes on the head, three thicker ones can be distinguished that, if it can be pulled out, serve as amulets, like the tagalog goblin wears a four-cornered bonnet. The serpent of the ancients also had three spikes on its head like the basilisk and the crowned devil of the Europeans. These details must have been embellished by the foreigners. The Bulislis and the Bibit are similar to the Tikbálang. The Bisayás call this one the Unglo. The Siúkuy is an anito of the river. the Mangmankik of the Ilocanos, punish with madness and other ailments those who treat a forest without respect or bathe in some unfrequented river. the pregnant ones, and with their tagalog name, it is confirmed that those Guardians of the weeds were men. Balo, other anitos of the depopulated. a colossal bird that nests in the clouds like the Ilocano Kúmaw: could it be the Mama. Well-known, symbol of shameless politicians. In Tayabas they have the timbabalak, a saurian little larger than a lobster with membranous wings that fold like a fan at their sides; This is what the Tayabeño Folk-Lore says. According to the Tagalogs, tremors are produced by the movements of an animal that exists in the bowels of the earth, as the Mountain Tribe's of Paragua(Palawan), Mindanao and Camarines think. This belief seems to be general in the Archipelago. The Tagalogs distinguish three classes of witches that are merged into a single witch in Ilocano: The Aswang, the Mananangal and the Mangkukulam, The Mangkukulam or Mangagaway is very similar to the Spanish witch, without a doubt imitated from is. She is a woman who has a pact with the devil, she cannot hold people's gaze, and in order to harm, she carries a doll that if she sticks a pin in the part that she wants to bother a person, it will cause intense pain there. According to Blumentritt, the ancient Tagalogs understood the Mangkukulam to be shrouded in flames. If it is true that such advice exists, it is analogous to the Mandarangan of the Bagobos, the anito of the volcano Apo, whose name seems to mean flaming or that catches flame Wouldn't that ancient Mangkukulam be the anito of the Taal volcano? But Noceda only says that he was a sorcerer. The Malays speak of a similar sorcerer who in Makassar is called Popokang manangala; in Menangkabaw, Palasík pananga; among the Battaks, Hantuen (that is, anito), and in Malacca, Penanggalang. The Aswang, according to the Tagalogs, is a Bisaya sorcerer (that is to say, this trickery must have come from there), it turns into a dog or a cat; he likes the liver of fetuses, and looks for it, even while in the womb. It is placed on the roof of the houses and from there it releases its tongue like a fine and long silk thread, but the night bird tiktik (spy against the Aswang) announces its presence to the people so that they can take precautions.That is why the sorcerer hates him to death and persecutes him.The ancient Tagalogs spoke of other sorcerers called Alasip or Atasip, and Ikki in addition to the Mathusalem Tagalog, the Hókloban sorcerer, who is also known by the Katanduanes. The Bataans also worshiped the Anitos and kept small pictures of them. Mindoro, Marinduque and Luban" The inhabitants of these three islands, wrote Fr. Martinez de Zúñiga in 1800, in their language, in their houses, furniture, clothing, boats, uses and customs, are in everything similar to the other Indians of the Tagalog nation. "Of which they are a part. The Christians have the same superstitions as the Tagalogs, and the Gentiles the same religion that they professed before being reduced to Christianity. They will worship an invisible entity that they call Anito, whose name they also give to the sacrifice that is made to him; The nono, which means grandparent, is respected and revered by alligators, large trees, rocks, and the tips of rivers and seas; tik...tik .they have priestesses to make their sacrifices that they usually consummate with a pig, which is distributed giving the best portion to the babaylan or sacrificer, they revere some birds, they believe in the immortality of the soul, and at the same time all superstitions believed by the ancient gentiles of these islands". Among the anitos of the Mountain Tribe's of Mindoro, called mánguianes, Malagia, anito of the rain, is cited.

CHAPTER 17
TEMPLE OF THE BICOLANO'S

I t is the same cult of the souls of the grandparents, who were called indistinctly Anuos or Diuatas, because the Bicolano's are the intermediates between those of Luzon and the Visayas; and they made wooden images of them. Until now, the peasants recognize Apo as God, according to the illustrated Filipino writer Pió Mondragon, FolkLore Tayabeño (1886), and Apo means nothing more than Grandparent. Fr. Castaño in Volume I of the Archive of the Filipino Bibliophile of Mr. Retana, taking* data from Fr. Lisboa's Bicol Dictionary (1865) that he seasoned with the news that Fr. Francisco de San Antonio had copied from Quirino and San Agustin invented a fantastic theogony for the Bicolano's, making us believe that Gugurang was their supreme god, when he was nothing more than a family Anito, whose idol the Bicolano's carried with them, and Fr. Lisboa assured that "if they asked him for rain, then it rained, and whatever else they asked of him, he did." He also invents a ghost that he calls Popó. But according to the Bicolano's, that ghost that prevents children from growing up is the Isaw. The classification made of the gods in Bathaias, protectors of peoples, and Katamhay protectors of individuals, and the other division of the gods, is inaccurate. Anitos, in Tagne, domestic genius; and Pararangpan, public benefactor or guardian of the people. The only thing that Fr. Lisboa says is the following: Bathala, according to the Bicolano's, was an Anito who made the one he accompanied happy and prevented misfortunes from befalling him. It was not a bird, Katambay is not found in his Dictionary, but I think it was Badhalang Katutubo himself, God and congenital protector of each individual. Tagne was an idol or figure of Anito. the memory of the dead. Langdon was an idol to whom the Balianas (bagans, priests) made sacrifices. Landong in Bisaya is the shadow, soul of the dead, or indigo. For this reason, the images of the anitos were called Landong. Dauani was a great weaver woman, and it seems that they believed that the rainbow was woven by her, since they call it Habul or Dauani (Dauani means weaving). This woman reminds me of the fabulous old woman who, according to the Iroquois, is continually spinning on the moon, and it is the one that will appear in the shadow of the tree that can be seen in it. Okot is another family anito who spoke to them whistling. the same Tikbalang that without a doubt would be the deceased of the enemy settlements or towns. It is not true that the Aswan is their King as the new Ahriman; he is not even a spiritual being, but a witch man or (122J ISABELO of the zoanthropic kings, of those monomaniacs who thought they had turned into animals and ate human flesh, nor is it exact that they live in hell, since the Bicolano's , like all the other Filipinos, they have no word corresponding to hell, nor a clear idea of it. The word Gagamban that Castaño cites as corresponding to hell, is not found in the Bicol Dictionary, nor is it found in the Oriol, Gulanggulangan and Columba Dictionary. We have discovered that the Kasanaan, which Fray San Antonio cites, was a misinterpretation of what Fr. Noceda had written in his Dictionary when he said: Kasanaan means nothing more than a crowd, thus kasanaan nang hírap (crowd of sorrows), is hell, and kasanaan nang toua, (crowd of joys) is heaven. As Blumentritt was wrong to write that the hell of the Ilocanos was called Kasanaan, only because I had written that in Ilocano sanaang means acute pain of the wounds .Zoanthropic advice made them believe in Lake, an animal found in the mountains with the feet and hair of a goat, and the face of a man. It reminds of Apo-Laki, an anito that the Pangasinans invoked when they went to war. The ancient Visayas, when they left their houses, invoked their little ones saying: Laki-Laki. The natives, from the island of

Flores (Atlantic) call their god KaLaki-Laki, The Bonggos were men who cast sparks of fire through their eyes, according to the peasants. They believed in Mañgindara, human-shaped fish that live inside the sea, and in Añgoñgool, an animal like a big monkey that walks in the rivers, hugs the person it finds and does not let go until herbs grow in the bones (which seems to cause death, according to the council.) *Bakunawa* is the fabulous animal that wants to swallow the moon in eclipses. In tag. Loko. *Irago is a very* large and highly painted serpent, mentioned only in the songs. It would be one of the great snakes that abound in the Philippines, and since they could not conceive where the soul of the man who devoured it would go, they would believe that it embodied in it, *Sarimaw*, a fierce animal, perhaps the tiger, just like the halimaw of the Tagalogs.   *Koró -koró,* bird is similar to the turtle dove, of ill omen.   *Atang* is to offer the priests food to the little ones, and then they eat it. It is   the   same   panangyatang   Ilocano. *Hogot,* was to sacrifice a slave for the death of a principal. *Himoloan*   the   tax   or   charge   of   a   thing. *Dool* abstinence from some foods due to the death of a relative.   *Sorague* song of the belianes. *Hidhid* the one who had a live locust or aphid on his body. *Yahod* superstition that was made with children, going around   inside   the   house   as   in   procession. *Sakom,* an ancient rite that consisted of whipping with banay leaves an insane or sick person who was believed to have lost his spirit, so that he could recover. Also, the Tagalogs and even the Spanish peasants whip with a thorny branch the sick who believe they are possessed by some sorcerer, so that he will leave. The active Bicolano's, like the other Filipinos, spoke of a fabulous bird, lord of the bats.

CHAPTER 18

THE BISAYAN GODS

It was the same as that of the Anitos, since this religion extended to Mindanao, where it is still preserved among the Mountain Tribe's. The Visayas, like the Bicolano's, call Kalag the soul; to the spirits of their ancestors, Umalagad, which seems to mean Keeper or Protector, and Landong to the shadow and idols of the diuatas. They practiced Shamanism no more nor less than the Itnegs of Abra now follow it, as we have seen in the Legazpi Report to the King of Spain before arriving in Manila. And they called *Tinodlok* the pig with signs to be sacrificed. Father Encarnación says: The ordinary victim is a pig, black to the hoof, killed beforehand skinned and gutted. They decorate him with leaves and put him on a small table called golang-golang. Around dances the high priestess is called Babaylan, and if she is a prophetess, they call her Catoólan. They call the minor priestess Daitan. Whom helps the sick (they regularly do these ceremonies with the sick) on horseback with a pig. they throw their harangue, they make their potions to the Devil (He was referring to his god, the Diwata: but the Romanists they always call the devil who is not that of their divinity, as if they were the only children of God) and then they eat the pork. To this ancient religion were added beliefs imported by the Malay Hindus and Mohammedans. Visayas islands, as in Mindanao and Paragua, upon the arrival of the Spaniards, the Anitos were more commonly called Dewatas, from Devalas or Devas, the same Guardian's protectors of the Hindus. Diuwata or Djewata to their spirits, angels or tutelary Guardian's. Also, the Malays of Borneo, Java, Sumatra call their spirits Dewata, Rewata, Djuwata or Djewata, angels or tutelary Guardian's. The Mohammedan maguindanaos designate a goddess by the name of Deioa, and dewata to the gods and idols of strangers. According to Fr. San Agustin, among the Visayas, dia means God; perhaps he meant Diua or Dewa,

The Visayas, like the Luzonics, worshiped the souls of dead fetuses or infants, like Anitos children, pa recited to the little angels of the paintings of the Romanists, or like pygmy Guardian's (Patianak, tag. and kibaan, iloc.) and they were called kuku (dwarf) or pandak and it seems that the Mohammedans turned him into Pandak Sitan or Saitan, or the dwarf Satan. The fact is that the ancient Visayas spoke of a Pandakesite that takes the souls to the Sulad or Pülag from which they had to leave through sacrifices. According to Blumentritt, the ancient Visayas called the god of hell Sumpoy. As a good Catholic, he also caught the habit of calling the gods of our grandparents the devil and the god of hell, which is certainly characteristic of a man of science like him. Sumpoy, must come from the root apoy or apuy (fire) and mean fire ring or some volcano. What is certain is that the Visayas did not have a word corresponding to hell. Father Encarnación in his Bisaya Dictionary writes: *Hell(infierno)*, lugar   nga   pasaquetan   (place   of   punishment). *Solad*,   entrails   of   the   earth,   tomb. *Suladmon*, deceased, inhabitant of the tomb. Sulad, then, was not like hell, but like an underground world where souls go, not precisely to suffer, as our brothers, the olo ngadjus of Borneo say of the good as well as of the bad like the Philippine Carón of which Aduarte spoke and Lisbusauen takes the souls to the Paradise that they placed in Borneo, which indicates the origin of these exotic beliefs. Only in the Mythological Dictionary of the wise Blumentritt have I read this. More in that of Fr. Incarnation that deserves us more credit in this matter, we do not find the names of Sumpoy, Maguayan or Lisbusauen, nor even Uatangau, which is undoubtedly a mistaken transcription of Balangau, since formerly the

Spaniards wrote with u and b as hauian instead of habian. The Aswang is Bisaya, and not Luzonic, as the Tagalogs claim right now. According to Blumentritt, it is the oldest name for the Malay devil in Dutch Malaysia. It is known by the Mandayas of Mindanao and other islands of the South. Baua is a bird, which, it is believed, was formerly an aswang that was transformed. The Ngio-ngio, was another witch that turned into a bird. Mángalo or Mangalok was similar to the Aswang as soon as it invisibly devoured the entrails and they attributed to it all death that was not due to old age. They sacrificed animals to him, even slaves, so that he might content himself with the entrails of the victims and leave the sacrificers alone. What was the name of the supreme god of the Visayas? Those of Limasaua, according to Pigafetta, called God Abba. According to Quirino, they designated the most supreme ancient god Laon. According to Father Delgado, which is what the people of the island of Negros called the Bisaya God who lives in the Malaespina or Kanlaon volcano, to whom they recommend their fields, since he is the one who sends locusts and other calamities. The Bataks of Sumatra called Si-Laon the anitos of their most ancient ancestors and among them it also means "ancient." Those of Panay had Sidapa as their god, creator of all things, who lived on Mount Maidas in Iloilo, which was his ologan (Paradise). From there he measured the virtues of all those who were born, who, once they reached their respective limit, died irretrievably. It seems that Sidapa is Laon himself, since this name is nothing more than a qualifying name. Talonanon or Tagalabong, to whom they asked permission to penetrate forests and mountains. To Naguined, Makbarubak and Aropayang, they asked that death, illness or some misfortune befall their enemies, Makaptan or Kaptan lives above Heaven, he also sickens and kills. *Makabantog* the diwata of scandal, and *Mábosog* the one who fed up, they were the main ones in the Araut river, coast of Panay. *Labawdumgug*, hero of his antiquity, was invoked in weddings and songs. In Iloilo, a certain rock that looked like a Bisaya was pointed out as his image. with his cane he propelled a boat. *Banog* (means hawk) was another rock in the shape of this bird; They said that he prevented the passage, if they did not venerate him and pay some present. *Simuran, Siguimarugan and Ramalay* were bad little boys, like Ogima, a demon transfigured into a satyr. *Todtod*, is a very big little boy with two teeth on top and two on the bottom; he has a stone arm, *Ratao*, a sea monster in a human figure halfway up and repeats what he hears. *Hanan*, anito or hero who gave them the rules of mourning. *Amakaudor*, another diwata of the ancient Visayas. According to a manuscript from the year 1580 that serves as the first appendix to the History of the Philippines by the Jesuit Delgado, the Bisayás or Pindos were divided into seafarers or beach dwellers, called higuecinas, and Mountain Tribe's, called tinginanes. According to the former, heaven and earth had no beginning; They had two gods: Kaptan and Maguayan, the wind of the land and the wind of the sea got married; the first wind spewed out a reed: this was planted by Kaptan and having grown, it burst, throwing out two little pipes that had a man and a woman: the male was called Sikalak and hence the name lalak to all men and to the woman, Sikabay, whence came the name babay given to women. The man proposed to the female that they marry because there were no others on the earth; but she opposed it because they were siblings out of the same reed without having been between them more than a knot. At last, they agreed to go to consult with the Earthquake, and he declared that it was necessary for them to marry, since there were no others in the world. later a daughter named Saman, These two brothers had a daughter Lubluban who married the son of the first men called Pandaguan, These two had Arion as their son, Pandaguan being the first inventor of the fishing pens; and The first thing he caught was a shark, he took it to land not thinking that it would die, and seeing him dead, he began to make offerings and cry to him, complaining about the gods, because until then none had died. He sent a messenger to find out what the dead man was, and not taking chances he sent a second messenger, which said again that it was a shark. Kaptan and Maguayan, angry that they had made offerings to a fish, Pandaguan killed with a lightning bolt and he spent thirty days in hell or the place of the dead, and at the end of them , they felt sorry for him and resuscitated him returning to the world, During his absence, his wife Lubluban fell in love with Marakoyan, and this was the first case of lovemaking, When Pandaguan arrived at his house, he did not. she found out because she had been invited by Marakoyan to eat a pig that she had stolen (this was the first robbery.) She sent her son to call her; but she refused? saying that the dead never return to the world» Then he turned angrily to the place of the dead. If she had attended the call and Pandaguan had not returned to the tomb, all those who died would return to the world. Everything was the fault of another Eva. The Tinginanes or Mountain Tribe's, according to said manuscript, had the following legend, the same one that Colin brings, whose origin we ignored until here, (Rectify what was said on page 31.) There was nothing but sea and sky. A kite, having nowhere to perch, stirred up the sky and the sea. The latter attributed it to the sky and declared war on it by swelling upwards. The sky punished it by throwing upon it these islands of the Archipelago to tame it and made the sea run from one part to another so that it could not swell again. From here came the Mavario, which is revenge for an injury, a common thing in this land. The kite bit a cane and from it the first man and woman came out. This one was called Kariuhi, and the first time she gave birth, she gave birth to so many children together, that the father entered the house very angry, and threatening the children, they fled in fear, some entering interior rooms and were later the main ones; others in outer rooms, and they were the timauas; those from here, in the dindines or cane walls, and were the slaves; those over there in the kitchen, and it was the blacks; and others went to sea, and they are Europeans and other foreigners. Although they lacked permanent temples, they had their offering houses or altars of ñipa called olango, and for great festivals or sacrifices, they improvised a palapala or cane construction adorned with foliage and flowers, as when giving thanks for a victory, etc. The hill of Pangibalón was the most notable of its shrines and the Spanish chroniclers assure that the diwatas answered their questions there. In cases of illness the sacrifices were made in the house of the mourner.

CHAPTER 20

THE DEITIES OF MINDANAO

Deities of Mindanao have been influenced heavily by the Moors & Mandayas due to their proximity to the oldest mountains on the eastern coast of Mindanao, they call the idols of their ancestors or the invisible beings, such as the Manobo's, diwata or manaug. They speak of God the father Mansilatan from whom the busaw emerges, a virtue that gives value to the Baganis (leaders), and of a God son, Badla. They invoke them in their diseases especially in headaches, epilepsy and paralysis. In these cases, the belians (priests) wound the idols of the evil Guardian's, dancing and singing that Mansilatan will descend from heaven and Badla will fix the earth. They have true demons: Pundaugnon, which means "tempter," and his wife Malimbog, who seduces and deceives men. On the other hand, among the Bagobos, Busaw means devil or bad diwata, the Bagobos, Malibod which must be the same, is a good diwata, protector of women. soul, spirit or spectrum. In eclipses, they believe that a dragon or snake wants to swallow the sun or the moon and shooting their arrows, they shout: "Let yourself be seen", grandparent (Pagkabaton, we offer prayer.) They have Kukú, a dwarf, like the Kibaan's or Patianak of the Luzonians; and birds of ill omen like the limokon and they believe, like the Tagalogs, that the tremors are caused by the movements of a large pig, baybulan, which rubs its body against the trunk of the earth to scratch itself. They consider Abdalian gods, their wife Kagabian and Paliti who lives on the summit of Mount Kampalili, where, according to them, there is a lagoon enchanted with alligators, turtles, sharks and other fish, which turn those who dare to go there into stones. Bagobos, their early religion was that of the Anitos or

Diwatas, as they are called. The god of good principle is Níto, according to Dr. Schademberg. They speak of Tagadium and Lumabat who were pious men and ascended to heaven with a swarm of white bees. Then God made little children for them and enlarged the sphere of the world, which he had made narrow. With the introduction of the Hindu avatars, they made Tagadium a God who became humanized with the name of Lumabat. Reminds Lumawig of the Montese Luzonians. They also have a trimurti similar to that of India, made up of three brothers: Tiguiama, good god, In the Bagobo-Spanish Dictionary of the Jesuit Mateo Gisbert, Manila 1892, They find the names of Malibud, Tagadium, Lumabat, Macoret, Macaponquis Mámale, Aóac, Camalay, Calambusan, Tagamaling, Maline, Saliéud Tomulac, Panayangan, Camaragan, Mandarangan, or Matuga guinaua who fosters the creative power; Manama who preserves, rewards and punishes; and Todlay who presides over marriages; according to others, he is the creator of men. At weddings they offer him buyo and rice. Todlay has Todlibong as his wife, always a virgin, who dwells in heaven, is like the wife of Brahma, or Maya, mother of Buddha, who imitated the pagan Christians committing the enormity of marrying Mary with the Spirit of God. the Abba of whom Pigafetta spoke; to Kamalay, siring who is the anito dwarf, as an elf; to Kalambusan and the giant Tagamaling, (the Malin of the subanos). According to another author, the main god of the Bagobos is Mandarangan, God of the Apo volcano. His heart is called Matuga-guinawa (good heart) and they pay special homage to it, which recalls the heart of Wishnu that the Jesuits have imitated in the Sacred Heart of Jesus or can the Bagobos ascend to said volcano without sacrificing a man, whose blood they offer for drink. He has several wives, which seems to indicate a Hindu-Mohammedan origin; perhaps it is a reminiscence of Agni Hindu deity of fire; according to others, the Apo volcano is the mouth of hell, a belief that must be imported from Java. Other gods are Panayangan and

Totnulak, according to Blumentritt, and they speak of
Makoret, creator god of the air; of Makaponkis, creator of
water; of mammals,[13] creator of the earth; of Malibud,
creator of women (is it the same Malimbog?); of Kamaragan,
god of married women; of Salibud, who taught the first men
to cultivate the fields, trade, and carry on industries; of
Kantbulan, his Adam , and of Bayguebay or Beiguebei who
was his Eve or first wife They speak of the demons
Kalambusan, Pelubatan and Tabankak who induce lust, fights
and murders so that his master Rioarioa eats, This is a
monster that hangs at the zenith like a pendulum, he devours
men with his tongue, like the Aswang or the Balbal, who is his
sorcerer. The Balaitan is a sorcerer. The Maguindanao Moors
call the devil lilis. Tambara is a little house with plates
dedicated to the diwata and that is also the name of the frame
for the diwata, which each wealthy person has. Gisbert says
that God is Diwata in bagobo, and he always speaks of Diwata
and not diwatas in the plural. Almost all of this must have
been imported. The net was the cult of the apos or
grandparents, keep the Mandayas and Bagobos in their
diwatas as protectors, such as the Tagbalay anito of the house;
the diwata Tagtabibi, protector of children; the Tagalanua,
anito of the earth or of the fields; the Tagalaílaw, anito of good
weather; the Darago, which is reminiscent of the Trago de los
Bicolano's, causes illnesses or sheds blood; but according to
Gisbert, on the contrary, he is the diuata of courage, and they
invoke him at their festivals. Tirurays, evidently kept their
true religion which was the cult of their ancestors. Laguey-
Lengkuos Laguey-Bidekkroon, Laguey-Feguefedan, Laguey
Lindib-lugatu and Laguey-Titay beleyen, were Priests in life,
but are now venerated as Saints. Laguey means King; it seems
to correspond to the Lakan in tagalog. L. Lengkuos married
the virgin Metiatil and without getting together, they created
Matalegu ferrendam. The Fenebang had been people who
turned into animals for having disobeyed Laguey-Lengkuos
the angel ag belalá or ketrekam are also deified men. Until

now they call the invisible beings diwata, but especially the fabulous fish with eight heads that lives in the navel (center) of the sea. And we know that diwata means anito or soul of the Apos (grandparents). One of them is called Opo-Luke an evil genius. Opo means brother, and Lukes corresponds to the Ilocano Dákes, which means bad, demon. Telaki is good diwata, angel which is the Apo-Laki soul called kamatu and it seems that they distinguish several denominations of the soul in a man. The Fagad is a goblin that eats the dead like the Bolbol or Balbal, a sorcerer who causes diseases and devours the entrails of the corpses. For this reason, the tirurays put a mirror on top of the corpse so that the Fagad flees in fear, seeing two heads with a single body or believing that his soul is guarding the corpse. They call God Tulus, perhaps the name of the main ancestor of the tribe. The Bataks of Sumatra and the Olo-ngadjus of Borneo say that the land rests on a snake or dragon called Naga-padoja or Naga-pusah (snake of the earthquake), and when it moves, it produces tremors. Other times they say that this snake is a man, perhaps Angngaló or the Atlas that supports the earth. Naga is the same fabulous serpent entity among the Hindus. According to Blumentritt, the monster fish of the tirurays is also called Naga, they have the Bulalutalun diwata of the forest that eats human flesh. They speak of Bongos, like the Bicolano's, and they have Bongo-watir-atir , a maiden who ascended to heaven and Bongo-solo-delemon another demigoddess, and other kenogons or deified virgins, such as Kenogon Enda and Afán, Enguelemon, Enguertayar, Sambuyuya, and Metiatil, who remained a virgin as the wife of Laguey Lengkuos Pilanduk, evil spirit; Semeligan, is the same Bolbol goblin but who appears pretending to be a relative or housemate who is absent; and they only know Saltan, the Sitan of the Arabs (Satan). They also call the devil Demangias, Mofirrou, God owner of the souls of the murdered, and with him they go to rest. The tirurays, after murdering someone, commend his soul to him by singing the kerreensiou. They have no word for hell. Belian is a priest, and Tenines is a neat little house where the Belians talk to God. The Bukidnons of Mindanaw call their gods Apo (grandparent) and invoke in times of war or epidemic the country anitos called Tauo sa sulap, like the Tauong-damó of the Tagalogs and the Talonanon of the visayas means wild men.

CHAPTER 19

GOD OF THE PARAGUA (PALAWAN)

T he Tinitians and the Tagbanuas they call diwatas to the anitos or invisible beings, good or bad. The superior god of the Tinitianos is Banua and in their deaths they beg him not to kill others. The Bulalakaweño's fear Mangalok and to drive him away they burn certain seaweed; Tawo-Satolonan, who must be the same Talonanon or rural genius of the Visayas, they say that he eats the children of heaven; Sedutnunadok, god of the earth, they invoke when they harvest rice; Magutndose, god of the mountains from which rivers rise, they invoke him in their needs and offer him rice and dried fish; Poko, god of the sea, winter they invoke to remove illnesses; and to Tabiakond, god of the interior of the Earth, which must be the giant or snake, whose movements produce earthquakes.

CHAPTER 21
ANITISM & SPIRITISM

Similarities of Anitism and Spiritism in the ancient Philippine religion are apparent, but if we separate the exotic additions, influences of the Hindus and Mohammedans, there was nothing more than the ancient Aniteria or Anitism, which served as background general to all religions and is none other than modern Spiritism, as we shall see in the following similarities:

1. Filipinos and spiritualist's believe in the existence of a semi-material soul, which the former call aningaas and the latter perispirit.

2. Anitist's call that soul anioaás or kar-karmá when the body is alive, and anito or kaloluat when the body is dead. Spiritualists call it soul when it is still attached to the body, and spirit when it separates from it.

3. Aniteros and spiritualists believe that this spirit can enter other living bodies.

4. They both agree that when baglans and mediums evoke spirits, become hard, ecstatic or frantic, Baglans and mediums are equally hysterical, visionary or hallucinated.

5. They agree in believing that not only living beings, but even objects, have a shadow or spirit, to which the spiritualist's attribute their cohesion, which they call affinity, to and that was the first form of Religion and Spiritism.

Similarities with Romanism:

1. Both say that the spirits come on the wings of the wind. The Filipino Anitos were nothing more than the Saints of the Romanists, deified men, in imitation of paganism.

2. The little angels of the Romanists in the form of newborn babies or just little heads, are similar to the semi-divinized souls of the fetuses.

3. Anitist's and Romans believe in anitos or evil Guardian's, who are the demons of the past.

4. Both believe in supposed appearances of the soul after the death of the body; or apparitions.

5.

They believe in witchcraft and in the efficacy of exorcisms.

6. Both have idols or sacred images of human Philippine Religion fell into the same errors as Mosaicism, Romanism, Protestantism and Spiritism, because of the imperfection of its scientific knowledge ; but it is as holy and worthy of our deep respect, as all other Religions, in its object, that is, in its natural instinct to seek the true God to pay him the tribute of our adoration and gratitude for his inexhaustible and providential mercies. Other similarities Buddhism also has as its background the divinization of man. And Brahmanism professes other common beliefs. Anitism has great similarities with all other religions, since it is the one that served as the general basis for all of them. I believe that Anitism is indigenous and the first form of religion. The foundational system that existed in all countries.

CHAPTER 22

LEGENDS OF THE PHILIPPINES

When the reason of ancient man became clear, he suddenly found many things for him inexplicable: the day with the clarity, the night with its darkness, the sky with its stars, the air with its clouds, winds, rains and lightning; the sea and the rivers with their fish and amphibians; the earth with its volcanoes, its animals that sometimes look like sphinxes, and the plants that, although immobile, sprout and grow, sometimes give off sounds when shaken by the wind, and at night they seem to be the dwellings of invisible beings with the songs of orthoptera or with the light of fireflies or fatuous fires; and when he began to make observations, he noticed that those who entered the forests or swamps died of fever, not knowing that it is produced by the humus of the virgin forests or by the microbes of the swampy places, such as the rice fields. At first none of this called his attention, except for the imposing roar of lightning and of the volcanoes that instinctively overwhelmed him with fear; He believed that everything was natural, that everything was born and developed, like a grass that sprouts spontaneously from the earth. He did not even notice the need for a creator. Kaffirs still believe so, as Burchel attests in Travels; And if you press questions about the origin of these things to the most ignorant of our mountains, they will answer the same thing: that everything is because yes, everything is natural! and spontaneous; who knows nothing of the first cause. Man, then, seemed to begin with an innocent religious idea of the supernatural; but being instinctively afraid of the noise of the phenomena of Nature, he soon began to find out what living beings were hidden in them and tried to disarm his rigor by offering them his food, which was the best he had. His rich imagination gave him what he wanted, confirmed his fourth suspicion, and his mere suppositions became beliefs and then dogmas. Little by little the man-child began to focus on what affected him most closely and directly hurt his feelings. As indifferent as he was, the violent interruption of life in his loved ones could not help but deeply affect him and make him meditate. How could people absolutely die who only yesterday or a moment ago spoke to us and loved us dearly? The affection thus mortally affected, combined with his dreams in which he would again see and speak with people already dead, made him think that there is something more in man than the body that is corrupted by death. He observed that in the sleeping man (who is the image of a dead person), while the body sleeps, usually his anger remains awake and wanders through mysterious or unknown regions. He united this with that shadow that, similar to his own, follows him everywhere, a shadow whose reality becomes visible in a surprising way when one looks at oneself in the mirror of the waters, or in the will-o'-the-wisp that sometimes comes out of tombs, and his belief was strengthened that there is another man inside each man, what our Ilocanos call aningaas, anioaás or kar-karmá in tagalog, kakap, and kamatu for the Tirurays. That aningaas, that shadow, they believe that it is an emanation of the body, it is formed from the vapors that perspire through our pores; therefore, although it seems impalpable, in reality is visible. This aningaas is the reason and the shadow; thus, the madman has lost his aningaas or his shadow. Like the American Indians and the ancient Greeks, they believed that the corpse does not have a shadow spirit either. When a peasant loses his reason, they accompany him to the remote places through which he is supposed to have lost his aningaas and they shout calling him and to prevent him from staying, distract him when they withdraw from the woods, they exclaim: Come on, come on![15] The testimonies of the visionaries and madmen who claim to have friends only visible to them with whom they talk continuously, and the healthy peasants believe that they actually have them, will have been decisive. Once we established the existence of aningaas or soul it easily occurred to man the idea of the other life or from the other mysterious world. Williams recounts that on a certain occasion he unexpectedly placed a handsome-faced Indian from the Fiji Islands in front of a mirror, and he became very happy, saying in a low voice: "Now I can see the spirit world" (Fiji and the Fijians). The man, because of his deep affection for his deceased, refused to believe in their absolute annihilation, and he thought that when the body died, his shadow would go to continue a life similar to the previous one, to that world mysterious to which it usually escapes during sleep man observed that other beings and objects even weapons and utensils have a shadow and he believed also have a soul, no doubt for the afterlife.[16] From this they deduced that the dead would follow a similar to this in the other world and for this reason they buried the dead with their weapons and work instruments according to the sexes, and they made the rich accompany them with slaves who they killed to serve them in the other life; and to the deceased they offered meals, whose substance they consumed. May have contributed to this ancient art & inscriptions that show us in space panoramas complete with man, animals, plants and instruments of work. Proof that ancient man is preserved in the jungles Philippines, is that the famous prehistoric tombs that date back to the Iron and Bronze Ages and even to the Neolithic period, are similar to those that our Mountain Tribe's make up to now. These prehistoric tombs are found in caverns or caves, or niches were opened in the same mountains or in dolmens or tombs with vertical stone slabs; above they were closed horizontally with other similar stones, and the interstices were covered with earth forming burial mounds. Inside these dolmens there are skeletons accompanied by utensils and weapons, such as crockery, polished axes, spear points, etc. I recommend that the societies of Anthropologists with students visit and excavate the caves, "In those of Tayabas, according to the enlightened folklorist Mr. Mondragon, they say that there is an enchanting cave that guards sphinxes of serpents, bulls charging with naked men and cornígeros. In Europe, similar prehistoric caves that preserve the first engravings and manifestations of art are highly esteemed. legendary mansions of enchanters that for me I add would be ancient cemeteries, and therefore, must be excavated under the direction of expert persons if on the outer shores of the Alabat Island and in Balogo (Camarines Sur) there are stretchers three spans long and 0.027mm skulls. in diameter."

CHAPTER 23

THE CULT ORIGIN OF THE PHILIPPINES

Philippine Mythology reveals to us the origin of the various cults, something that the sages were alligators and crocodiles unable to find due to lack of exact information, and where would ancient man think the soul goes after the death of the body? Reincarnation We said that a man devoured by an alligator, it was believed that his soul reincarnated in the amphibian, and for this reason, the Filipinos called grandparent certain alligators and crocodiles and so of the other animals, choosing as its totem or deified animal and protector the most feared in the region, such as the wild buffalo (cimarrón)[17], in whom they believed that the anitos used to incarnate, according to Aduarte; the wild boars, which are the ones that abound in the Philippines, and the alligator where there are, and where not, even the simple eels. For this reason, in the tombs that Sinibaldo de Más found among the Igorot's of Amburáyao, a carabao and a wild pig were engraved. And in other countries, where there are elephants, lions, tigers, special oxen such as the apis, bears, eagles and great apes, they are also preferred. The idea of reincarnation is almost universal among ancient peoples, Egyptian, Indian and even among the Greek philosophers. Plato admitted it, and Pythagoras even claimed to remember his previous existences. The Jewish philosophers profess this belief and call it gilgul; the same is true of the Manichean Christians and many modern ones. The Filipino Mountain Tribe's believe that the lightning sucks the brains of its victims and consequently, their reason or soul, which would be identified with the lightning; That is why they said that the one that thunders is their ancestors Kiruls, The lightning must not be such a fire, but man, because they say that by getting into the cane field, one sees himself free from it, because he fears being injured by the pointed leaves, Account Tanner in Narrative of Captivity among the Indians, that the common reaction of the red Indians, frightened by a terrible storm, offered tobacco to the thunder as if it were a man, asking him to stop. Lubbock continues, it is a general belief among backward races that thunder is the voice of a celestial or anthropomorphic deity Much later, when cars and the legends of the car of Helios or the Sun were invented, it was believed that thunder is the noise of that car, and lightning is the sparks that give off its tires when it collides with the cobblestones of the sky. If now the Ilocanos suppose that lightning at first is a white pig or rooster, this is an erroneous preservation of a belief. It is that when the thunder roars, he is hungry and asks for a pig or rooster of those that are usually sacrificed to the Anitos[18]. The souls of the drowned, according to the ancient Filipinos, 'remain in the water, and over time they are worshiped as Guardians of the liquid element. In the same way they believed that the spirits of those who were buried in their houses, they stayed in them, and these would be the Anitos of the house. The souls of those buried in the woods, who left populating them like country Guardian's, are called nunok (grandparent) to the baliti (Ficus), meaning that the soul of some grandparent lives in it. Trees were not venerated as gods, but as dwellings of the anitos, and from these come the vegetable and mineral talismans or amulets. would remain living in those mounds and others similar, such as the Nuno sa punsó (the grandparent of the mound). In Mindanao they call the volcano Apo (grandparent), proof that Mandarangan was a grandparent, perhaps devoured by its flames. Like an ancient Anito, La-laon lives on in the Malaespina of Negros volcano. Volcanoes inspired the idea of hell. As not all the dead were devoured by animals, lightning or water, it was necessary to imagine a mysterious world, where the generality would go to continue this life, and there was no other more appropriate than the deserted peaks of the highest or abandoned mountains. There the good ones went to receive their reward, having fun, singing, eating and drinking, which certainly must constitute the possible happiness, not only among Indigenous tribes, but among the most civilized as well, without stopping working, for which they carried their instruments of labor. The continual party would cloy and become a torment. And those who were bad, would try a new life again to see if they improved; but the pure, simple and good heart of the man-child could never believe in absurd hells, because with his admirable intuition he understood of course that the setbacks, sorrows and miseries of this life are enough to punish our weaknesses. "The penalty of fire in hell, says Grasserie, is rare, almost exclusive to the Christian religion,"* and it would be even more exact to say, of Neoplatonic Christianity, which is adulterated Christianity. The various hells must have This Christianity imitates Mazdeism, Brahmanism or Chinese Taoism. Life in the other world, for the Indigenous person, is like the present one: for the good, a garden of delights, and for the bad, miseries that can be remedied with sanctifying work, only when her intelligence rises or when she thinks of communion with her God, and becomes spiritualized even in her joys and sorrows. Transmigration Mirages, those frequent optical phenomena in the plains warm or in the sea, which consist of seeing panoramas reproduced in the air with their men, beasts and trees, which are at a distance from the spectator, inverted as in a photographic machine, I think they produced the idea that the souls of the deceased travel the air. From here I gave them. anitos verses of space; and that must also have opened the way to the idea of the transmigration of souls to stars. At first, they were not concerned with finding out who could have made the Universe, believing that everything arose spontaneously. Thus, in effect, many cultures have a different ideology other than that of a supreme of a Creator, such as the Indians of California, the Zulus, the Hottentots, the Bongos of the Sudan, the Siberians, the Cris of the Pole, the Australian Negroes, (and perhaps some of our mountains) according to the testimonies of Dobritzhoffer, Baegert, Stuhr, Muller, Callaway, Franklin, etc. Later, when the understanding of the race has succeeded in making gods of their ancestors, their rich fantasy as a child attributed to those ancestors extraordinary powers and came to consider them as builders of the Universe as the Basutos and West Africans believe, and for this to be possible, it was necessary to imagine that the progenitors were immense giants, as the Slavs, Germans , Hindus, Ilocanos, etc. and where he saw clefts in the mountains, he took them for the footprints of said giants, and the mountains themselves as benches or seats for them, and immense animals and reptiles, which now no longer exist. Here we have then discovered in the depths of Philippine Mythology as the various cults of phenomena, of giants, of animals, of serpents or amphibians, of plants, of the watchers, of the stone beings that were nothing more than images of the Anitos, etc. All had as their origin the cult of souls.

CHAPTER 24

THE CULT OF THUNDER, LIGHTNING, AND VOLCANOES

T he Cult of lightning, volcanoes and fires, In the history of the first civilized peoples (China, India, Persia, Chaldean-Assyria, Egypt, etc.) The first ordered cult that we find was that of the Sun but serving as a background vestige of ancient fetishism. That was, when man was already civilized, when he began to observe the stars, he discovered the great importance of the Sun as the center and source of all life in our piety system. But, as Voltaire observed, ancient man, like the child and the contemporary Indigenous person, must not even have noticed the true importance of the sun and for him it was nothing more than a lamp from the sky, whose size is that which it offers on the horizon when it rises or sets, so The hill people and peasants of the Philippines believe it. According to the Bible itself, the sun is nothing more than a lamp hanging from the solid vault of the sky, greater than the tiny stars. The Brahmins said that Fire was worshiped for being the image of the Sun; but it is not likely that the cult of Fire is later than that of the Sun. When the real importance of this star was discovered, only then was it unified with that of Fire still advancing it. If we delve into the histories In the Indies, the cult of Fire seems to precede that of the Sun. The name of Aloro, the first fabulous king that Babylon had, does not mean more than "god of fire before Belo, the King deified in the sun. According to the ancient Zen traditions, this cult originated from a spark when a stone was thrown against a rock. That is to say, when man discovered the property of silex of producing fire. It is possible. Before that, thunder and volcanoes did not. They would have ceased to fill ancient man with fear, and consequently, to be objects of his adoration. I believe that the cult of fire originated from the adoration of lightning, volcanoes, and fires, we do not know if it was simultaneous or earlier than the sun, but by no means after. The Jews called lightning "arrows of God" The cult of fire is ancient and almost universal. The Aino's, aborigines of Japan, have as their main God, not the sun, the moon, or the stars, but fire, from whom they ask for whatever they need, according to Bickmore.[19] The Tagalogs call the fire metaphorically pumpkin, squash or an incarnated vine and others consider it as a dragon of fire, whose multiple tongues make whatever they lick disappear. One of the ancient amulets was the cross that represented two canes that rubbed together, that led the fire; It was venerated as sacred by the Hindus, Persians, Babylonians and others. Later this ancient procedure of producing fire in the swastika or manji was perfected, also in the form of a cross, which was given by rubbing or drilling a hole in the middle. With this same sign was represented the sacred letter T, tau, which fifteen hundred years before Christ was worn as an amulet by Chaldeans and Egyptians.

CHAPTER 25

THE GREAT SUN CULT

I t must not be as old as the first believed civilized peoples. The engravings of this star found in some prehistoric tombs could have been nothing more than symbols or adornments, but not as objects of worship. (See them in the Philippine Bible p. III). It seems undoubted that man only deified the Sun, when he already had an idea of ultra-terrestrial life; thus, it is not prior to the cult of souls. For the Filipino Mountain Tribe's, it seems that the Sun and the Moon are nothing more than ancestors, as it is believed in Japanese Shintoism.[20] We have already seen how the Mandayas of Mindanao, when an eclipse occurs, shout and fire their weapons saying: "Grandparent, let yourself be seen". Some mountain people of Luzon make a fuss trying to drive away the dragon that wants to devour the aforementioned stars, which is also a Chinese belief; but this has been denied by those of Benguet. According to Morga, the Filipinos worshiped the sun and the moon, and Dr. Rizal, in his patriotic desire to extol our pre-Hispanic civilization, commented saying that the Sun was the supreme God of the Filipinos and that in Nature there is no other being greater and more admirable than said star. This comment of the Filipino immortal reminds us of the Inca of Peru who answered a missionary. "You invoke a dead God; I adore the Sun that never dies". But since our object is to investigate the pure truth, we now dispense with the patriotic and declare that the ancient civilized Filipinos venerated, in effect, sayings and other stars with the names of bathala in its meaning of beautiful lights and of mysterious origin. Right now, our mountaineers admire the sun and the stars as heavenly bodies and their images are tattooed on their forearms, but they ignore the important role that the sun plays in our planetary system. In a secondary way, perhaps this veneration (not worship) was introduced by the Japanese, Hindus, or Mohammedans. What Fr. Villaverde says that according to our Mountain Tribe's, the stars are the abodes of the gods, if that was true it would be possible to approximate their true magnitudes, and the reality is that for them the stars are sacred illuminations. The Ilocano legend that there is a sleeping Saint Joseph on the moon, or of a being residing there, according to the Igorot's, must be later than the prehistoric age we are studying. They adored the stars, judging by the Polynesians. Some Spanish authors say that the Ayta adore the Sun; but we have not been able to verify it. According to the first Spanish discoverers of the Philippines, "it does not seem that the Filipinos worshiped stars, animals, or skulls or other things that the Gentiles worshiped. (Memory of April 20, 1572). In any case, among our other Mountain Tribe's, the veneration of the Sun is very secondary in comparison to Anitism. Lord Kames in the History of Man states that the Malays of Borneo and Sulawesi have no other gods than the sun and the moon, that is inaccurate; they like our ancestors their brothers, professed Anitism as far as the memories of the most ancient peoples in civilization reach, the cult of the stars is intimately linked with the deification of the kings. In Egypt we saw that by flattery they compared their kings with the sun, for which they gave them the nickname of Pharaohs, In Assyria we saw that King Belo became a sun-god, as well as Mithras in Chaldea and Persia, and that, among the Zenda's and Hindus, their divine reformers metamorphosed in the star Sirius, the brightest star we see. It is possible that what began as a flattery of the kings comparing them with the brilliance of the stars[21], ended in Sabianism; that when the souls of the kings were deified, the stars were adored, as their abodes at the beginning; and later, when advances in astronomy demonstrated the great importance and influence of the sun and the other stars on earth, only then were they deified as such gods. Monotheism was born from the knowledge of the universal predominance or influence of the Sun on our planetary system, that is, on the then known Universe. The cult of the Sun began being ruffly for hot countries it is malefic, attributing to it sunstroke and other illnesses. And for the cold regions, he is a beneficent god.

CHAPTER 26
THE WIND CULT

We suppose that the wind is the breath of Anito, since in his Alas say that it comes to the baglan's. According to the Ilocanos who give him the treatment of Apo (Lord), he comes from some cane fields of the Abra, probably from a cemetery or dwelling of Anitos. spirit of the wind and of the rains, which shows that the wind is nothing more than the soul of some grandparent. The tirurays call the wind the sea, saying: Kemerrek! They imagined that the Creator had locked up the winds in caverns that they called the treasures of God. (Spinoza, Theological Political Treatise I, p. 41).

CHAPTER 27

ZOOLATRIA

The cult of animals is based on the reincarnation of the souls of the deceased and that those were venerated, not as such animals, but by the deceased reincarnated in them. The Greeks and Romans did not worship animals; but according to Plutarch, each god had his sacred animals: Aphrodite the dove, Apollo the raven, Artemis and the dog, etc., just as the Romanists give the four evangelists an eagle, a lion, an ox, and an angel, (which symbolizes the vision of Ezekiel I, 10.) Until now the Tirurays of Mindanao believe in reincarnation and speak of the fenabangs, people who became animals. In Guinea they believe that monkeys, crocodiles and snakes are reincarnated men. In Madagascar, the Betanimena tribe believe that the babacute, a species of lemur, is an incarnation of the spirits of their ancestors and are horrified to kill her. (Fork-Lore Record). In Sumatra (our brother country) they call the tigers nenek meaning ancestors, (nuno in tagalog, grandparent) to the tigers, being their real name rimaw (alimaw wild animal in tagalog) or machang (In Filipino, machín means "monkey"). They are afraid to call them by their names, like some of our countrymen due to their deities and parents, considering it disrespectful. Japanese legends tell that, persecuted by the daughter of a king of the Asian continent by her own father for incestuous purposes, she fled to Japan in a canoe with no other companion than a sacred dog and landed in Yeso. She had several sons who were demi-gods of the sacred dog Inu and were the parents of the Aino's, an aboriginal race that now occupies the northern part of Japan without merging with the Japanese, aino means sacred dog. Perhaps the name of the Inu dog had been given by the invaders to the aborigines because of their insecurities. This legend is a variation of the other, according to which the Japanese come from 300 young men and 300 maidens that the Chinese emperor Hoangti sent to the seas of Japan to seek the flower of immortality. In Japan it is believed that men reincarnate to become badgers or other canines (like foxes or dogs).

CHAPTER 28
THE CULT OF SERPENT

Some crocodiles and alligators were worshiped as reincarnations of our ancestors. Sometimes the Indigenous peoples of the Philippines believe that the spirits of the dead reappear in the form of large serpents and are distinguished by frequenting huts, they do not eat mice or fear men; Sometimes they even believe that they find in the serpent characteristic signs of the dead person who is supposed to have been incarnated in it and they usually offer them sacrifice or food. It seems that for the same belief the great snakes called boas were respected by the Filipinos, which they consider harmless unlike the others; they take care of them at home, feeding them. The Ilocanos speak of an island where, as the snakes grow old, they go to petrify. In Java they believe that sometimes a woman gives birth to a crocodile at the same time as a child. The Filipinos say it is a snake instead of a crocodile. Kaffirs believe that their ancestors hide in snakes, according to Casalis, Chapman, Callaway, Arbousset, Livingstone, and others. In Madagascar & Guinea the crocodile is considered a deity whose clemency they invoke in their prayers and songs, as an object of worship, the serpent is the first of all animals, according to Deane. It is widespread throughout the ancient world. Müller, in his Scientific Mythology, says that the snake symbolizes youth and health, according to the Gospel, prudence. Fergusson, in his book on the cult of the trees and the serpent, says that it was worshiped for its beauty; moreover, we believe with Lubbock that she was simply due to flattery, a manifestation of the Filipinos adoration. The Bakunawa of Bíkol and the Laho Tagalog are alligators and crocodiles that want to devour the sun or the moon in eclipses.

CHAPTER 29

PISCALATRIA

The Igorot's of Lepanto venerate eels because they believe that the souls of their deceased are incarnated in them. In Marianas they believe that the souls reincarnate in fish. The ancient Bicolano's spoke of the mangindara, fish that had human forms and they surely believed that the souls of some drowned had incarnated in them. The Tagalogs speak of the bulig fish that is kept alive in the stomach of the Mangkukulam. The Tirurays call diwata the fabulous cetacean Naga which according to them, lives in the "navel" of the sea and diwata means soul of the deified ancestor.

CHAPTER 30

AVILATRIA

The cult of birds is linked with the reincarnation of the deceased. In Japan, we often see in their dramas a deceased person reincarnated in a canary whose chirps are understood by the relatives of the deceased, or in a large black butterfly, Quite We have spoken of the tigmamanok bird. According to the Visayas, the baua was an Aswang man who transformed into a bird, and they greatly fear the kaskas, a very large nocturnal bird. It is probably the same fabulous kurnaw of the Ilocanos that picks up abandoned children, Ilocanos and Tagalogs speak of the adarna bird (a possible Spanish word) whose excrement turns anyone it touches into stone. The Igorot's and Mayoyaos speak of a bird whose excrement petrifies, according to Fr. Villaverde The truth is that the Filipinos did not worship birds as goddesses, but only as bringers of omens, such as the salaksak and kiring of the Iloc., the labég of the Mountain Tribe's, the kilitkilit of the Bulalakaweño's, the balantikis or balatiti (tag.), the saya-saya or beech of the Bicolano's, the limokon or league of the Mindanao (Phabotreron brevirostris). The raven cannot be master of the land except in so far as it is shameless; the Filipinos do not eat their meat because it disgusts them. Thus, their supreme god was most probably not the raven, as some chroniclers claimed.

CHAPTER 31
THE TREE CULT

As for Phytolatry or the cult of trees There was none in the Philippines and probably nowhere for that matter The lotus flower, the Egyptian plant, and the sacred Asclepias acida of India and Persia were symbols rather than anything else. De Brosses claims that the English word church comes from chercus (oak), which is already claiming. The trees were not worshiped as gods, but as the dwellings of watchers or anitos, such as the tibbeg of the Ilocanos, the baliti {Ficus índica linneo) the kalumpang {Sterculia foetida, Linn) according to Martínez de Zúñiga, and the bagaw, according to Buzeta and Bravo. According to Fr. Villaverde, the Igorot's recount that some of their deceased returned to visit the places and ranches of the living Igorot's; one of those tells that he came with his wife to visit his family, who supported them with the flower of rice flour. Tired and the relatives of treating them so much, they embarked on the journey with them going to one of the mountains of the Mayoyaos to the West of Kawayan in Isabela a province in Luzon.The man sitting on a rock and in the shade of a tree, the excrement of a bird that perched there fell on his head (This bird, whose excrement turns whoever it touches into stone, is called Adama, according to the Ilocanos and Tagalogs) and until this day he still sits there even the shape of his head can be seen. There is sacred trees found among the mountain people of India, in America, South Egypt and other parts of Africa, the Celts, the Lapps, those of Assyria, Persia and Greece, and even the Seneca, affirm that the veneration of trees existed but as abodes of the gods, In said points, as in the mountains of the Philippines, they hang little flags or adorn certain trees with rags to please the watchers that dwell in them, to make amends to them and ask for the lost health of those who suffer fevers. The Dayaks of Borneo believe that in the trees live anitos or souls that they call gana. These can get into the body of the living, and they ask permission to cut down trees, like the Filipino foresters. The bataks of Sumatra do the same, and they call these tree anitos tondi. They mainly worship the anito of the rice field. The Javanese venerate the baliti which they call waringi, and the Ceram alphas believe that their kings are descended from the baliti, like the ancient Filipinos, from the bamboo (Bambus arundo Linn.) In India and Sri Lanka, the bo tree is worshiped. Two hundred and fifty years before Christ, King Asoka sent a branch of bo and it was planted in the center of Sri Lanka from then on, it has been revered here as the first "sacred tree" of that island. The Polynesians hold the ava banana as sacred. The Ilocanos utilize the flower of the plantain or banana tree, when bowing to the ground, casts a shiny little stone, which is also used as a powerful amulet to those who provide talismans for the anitos of the trees like the Kibaan's etc. In Ogtok de Ragay (Camarines) a sacred forest is indicated that encloses the enchanted palace of an ancient one like that of Sukú in Arayat, and another mountain on the island of Alabat.

CHAPTER 32

AMULETS

Talismans, amulets, agimat etc. from the Arabic tilsam, means magical figure and Amulet, from the Latin amolior, to preserve (from evil). The mountaineers and peasants In the Philippines distinguish several kinds of talismans or amulets, which the Ilocanos call: taguiroot, the mysterious and rare plants that have virtues to attract love, etc. An Itneg sold me love & desire talismans that contained some plants and roots similar to hair. Babato or guin-guinammul and the prodigious little stones that enclose certain vegetables, reptiles, fish, birds or meteorites and have the power to make us invincible, invulnerable, invisible or to attract us the love of women, Both the taguiroot and the babato, must be fed with pure oil coconut or with milk. They also serve as certain amulets, fruits, seeds, or monkey bones which protect against illnesses and disease, or other animals also serve as amulets which have similar virtues. The mutya is the will-o'-the-wisp that they say comes out of the mouth of the extraordinary roosters and crystallizes into another amulet. The anting-anting, as its name indicates, is of Latin origin, and means anti or counter-dangers. All the aníing-anting that we have seen are Christian prayers written in Latin and, according to the same tradition, they were introduced as amulets by the Jesuits and friars. They are, not more or less, those prayers that Catholics use against the plague, etc. (samples of these Latin anting-antings are inserted in Martínez de Zúñiga's Estadismo, Appendix A). The Moors of Mindanao and Joló have similar talismans, but they are written in Arabic and according to the beliefs Mahomedans: they invoke Allah (God) and Mohammed his prophet saying among other things: "I trust in Allah Almighty to free me from Sitan (Satan) who was expelled from heaven, in the name of Allah clement and merciful. Note that Álah does not mean more than God and is the same Eloha of the Israelites, the Elah of the Babylonians, and the very God of the Christians and of the whole world. The sum is a potion, an antidote against poisonous bites; It reminds us of soma, the sacred wine of the Persians. The Tagalogs call the wild amatory vines gaytima, and mutiá, the little stones that serve as amulets; the pamaynan, and the saolopong are powerful pebbles; the galanan, talisman of Payabas, like the paadiokan, a monetary charm that brings great luck and abundance. The Germans have such a coin and call it heckep fenning. The galing, personal virtue; the one who has galing with only his word commands the snakes and performs other prodigies; the gaway, a spell; the golo, a love hex ; the hikap, a spell that kills instantly; the bating-tawo, another spell; the tagalpu weakens the contender; the taguibidag blinds him; the taguisama makes him hateful; the kabal, which means armor, a spell that prevents being wounded, in Bisaya Kibal and in Tiruray, Kebel. Amatorial or love spells are made from a plant called manibig. The Bisayás have the dalongdóng, herb to enchant, the abiog, wild boar tusk, the tagadlom, the panaglimatá, herbs that make us invisible; the daligmatá herb that summons an invisible sorcerer; the lo-may, amatory herb; the odong stupefies and leaves the enemy at a distance; the gapon spell; the alok, idem to cause diseases; takin, the kapinan shellfish, produces a bountiful harvest; taliakom, the good luck that certain weapons, tools of work, nets, cattle etc. carry with them. The paniyas is the same as the kibal, the inaw allows objects to be seen through water, land or something else. The tirurays of Mindanao have pebbles, shells, alligator teeth, pieces of wood, etc. That can provide whatever it is you desire or want, especially the love of women; the fallud tatnuk attracts foreign items; Afangelung louoj, shields the body against diseases and spells; the fangil that reveals whether one is wise or ignorant; the faro-manís that makes us beautiful; the fauden, hex that makes one sleep; the fekimoy that immobilizes the enemy; the felio makes the blow miss; the felunkang that calms the irritated; the fertrung makes us invisible; the ratnut bursts when it eats something stolen; the bongat kills the fruit thieves; fetetek, prayer, and the kambung another to calm storms; the ilemü and the kefit, other spells; the kemanbung stops the rain. The Moors have the adimat. The great Father of the Church, Saint Augustine, also spoke of an amatory herb called carissia.

CHAPTER 33
CULT OF POSEIDON

They are adored, not as animate beings, but as mansions of gods or deities. We said that the ancient Filipinos believed that the souls of the drowned remain in the water as genies of that body of water. Along rivers, they adorn the trees on the banks and when crossing them, they throw money or food like the offerings to our grandparents. Some bodies of water are believed to be inhabited by spirits that kidnap maidens; McMahon in The Karens of the Gold Chersonese. According to the Ilocanos, the anito of water also seduces and snatches unsuspecting young people. In Persia they consider the river Sogod sacred. In Sumatra they offer food and sweets[22]. The peasants of the Philippines are afraid of offending the sea, because it could drag them away, and the Ilocanos would not dare to pronounce the name of the Mermaid while they were in a river for anything in the world. The cult of the rivers prevailed in Europe and is preserved in mythology but as vestiges of mythology.

CHAPTER 34
CULT OF STONE MOUNTAIN

The cult of stones and mountains of which one wishes to be placed as an idol. In addition, the beliefs of our ancient ancestors believed that the rocks that have some resemblance to men, animals, birds or reptiles, had been before, but that they were petrified, simply by the old age as it is said of snakes, already by the excrement of a sacred bird. But always in the background is the cult of the deceased ancestor as a foundation. Remember what Aduarte said that the Kagayans not only believed, but also saw Anitos incarnate in the precious stone maxin. Our brothers the Javanese (Malays) preserve the following legend about the three rocks or statues of the Tjandi Mendut, which are near the Boro-Budur temple, the most remarkable monument of the Buddhists, which is supposed to date from the eighth century or 9th of A.D. Deua Kesuma, powerful prince of Java, offended a courtier. In revenge, he stole a two-year-old daughter. After twelve years, Deua Kesuma saw a young woman of singular beauty, and in love, he married her, having had a son. Then the offended courtier revealed to Deua that his wife was his missing daughter. Horrified, the father consulted with the bonzes (priests) and they told him that to purge the incest, either he had to shut himself up for the rest of his life between four walls with his daughter and the fruit of his mistake, or raise a sumptuous temple to Buddha without missing a single one of its images; and so he built the great temple of Boro-Budur; but since an image was missing, the gods turned him and his two sons to stone, and now the three statues of the Tjandi Mendut are shown to make incest abhorrent. touched the excrement of the prodigious bird Adama, like the Labawdungug of Panay, and worshiped at the

Banog rock that looked like a hawk, believing that these rocks had the success of the trips, like the natives of Vancouver Island. The Ilocanos say the same about some rocks in LákayLákay. In Sumatra and other Malay countries they have sacred stones, in Micronesia they worship stones, and the main divinity of Tokelau took a body made of stone. In the Fiji Islands there are sacred stones but are considered as rooms of deities. This cult was very widespread in the ancient world. The Phoenicians and Arabs practiced it, and the Hebrews also. In America and India, they worship in stones. In the latter, they paint them red and call them Pandus. According to Dulaure, the French continued to worship in stones even after the introduction of Christianity, and until now in some valleys of the Pyrenees (Succinct History of the Celts). Greeks and Romans venerated certain standing stones under the names of Hermes or Mercury. Dulaure thinks that the cult of the stones originated from the almost sacred respect with which those that served as landmarks were kept, which Lubbock adheres to; but we who know the fresh legends of this cult, know that they are far from the truth. They worshiped them, either as idols or fetishes, or as dwellings of the spirits, like the stone of Jacob called Beth-El, house of God. And as for the mountains, they were worshiped as the mansions of anitos or deities, or because of the sacred imprints engraved on them.

CHAPTER 35
CULT OF THE GIANTS

T
he cult of the giants. Sir John Lubbock does not mention it; but we find it closely related to that of the rocks and mountains, where it is said that there are footprints of immense human feet such as those of Angngaló, the man's boot darin of China, and the imprint of Budha. Regarding this we saw very gigantic statues in Japan and in Colombo, ancient cultures believed that the first men were giants. According to the German and Slavic Folk-Lores, Adam and Eve were giants. The same Bible asserts that giants existed on earth. (Genesis VI 4) In Europe we saw two giants: one Australian and the other Aragonese. The tallest Filipinos would only reach his shoulders. Currently there is in Cebu, according to the press there, a giant Bisáyá, Vidal Arellano, from the Tuburan police who is 2.25 meters tall, and the width of his body is 75 centimeters. If huge fossils of mammoths and other extinct gigantic animals are preserved, why would it be difficult for giants to exist? But fossils of giant men are not preserved. We repeat: the assumption of their existence must have obeyed first of all that there were gigantic animals; second, because of those cracks that look like human footprints; and third; because believing that the creators were our ancestors, they could only build the Universe, having extraordinary proportions. In the background, the cult of the ancestors always remains. I have already expressed my humble opinion that the Angngaló Ilocano must have been the same King of the creation, as Mr. Ponce said, or of Tagalicia, as I suspected. Later, going back to register the Folk-Lore Tayabeño of Mr. Mondragon, I found the following legend, which I have also heard, and I seem to remember that Rizal inserted it in one of his

novels. Mondragon says: "When three eights were gathered at the end of this year (1888), the enormous colossus, larger than that of Rodas, the Indigenous king now deposed and shackled, must have come out of the mount of San Cristóbal (Tayabas). The only thing left free is the little finger, which as it moves, the earth suffers horrific convulsions and lightning appears, then the Philippines will be independent. This legend is interesting, because it confirms the existence of a giant Tagalog king who is related to earthquakes and one foot of about two-thirds of a rod. Others say that similar footprints are found in the Norzagaray river (Bulacan) and on a mountain in Santiago (Ilocos Sur), that is, not as large as the Abra one.

CHAPTER 36

OFFERINGS AND SACRIFICES

Offerings and sacrifices are consequences of anthropomorphism or the belief that gods are like men with their needs and passions. The mountain people offer them food, because they suppose that they "need to feed." seem intact, but dull and without substance. So do the limbus who... live near Daryiling, according to Campbell. (Trans. Eihn. Soc.) The Filipino Mountain Tribe's also offer victims to their children so that they may be content with them and spare the life of the sacrificers. Then the offering becomes an atoning sacrifice. But we did not conceive of any other expiation than repairing the damage caused and doing charitable works for our faults with a firm purpose of amendment. In Peru, when one fell dangerously ill, one of their children was sacrificed to the Sun, begging it to accept the exchange. In Florida, as among the ancient Semites, all the first-borns were sacrificed to that star. We suppose that the legislators or the priests, in order to avoid aggression by others, ordered the sacrifice of their own son, of the first-born, as first fruits with it, like the Filipino Mountain Tribe's without a doubt because they suppose like the Hebrews that blood is the life or spiritual part of the bodies. Tanner relates that the Algonquians do not break a single bone of the victim, as the Gospel says they did of Jesus. Everywhere the victim or offering is held sacred. Sacrifice means to make sacred what is offered. Hence it was identified with the same divinity, like the Apis bull of the Egyptians, the sacred wine of the Hindus and Persians (the wine of Asclepias acida), the round discs of the sun worshipers, and the Roman halo that it was imitated from those discs. Among the mountain tribes of the Philippines, as in China and India, after the victim is offered to God, the priest distributes it among those who attend. The eccentric cultures offer the slaves of a conquered peoples who do not embrace their religion, so that they may have servants in the afterlife. Furthermore, as it was believed pleasing to offer animals and food to the gods, prisoners of war sacrificed them, as some cultures of Brazil and the Hebrews of the Bible practiced; Lev. XXVII, 28 and 29. The Assyrians offered human victims to the god Nergal; the Phoenicians to Moloch; the Romans continued to sacrifice men until 46 years after Christ, despite having prohibited it in 95 B.C. In Gaul the same thing was done. Human sacrifices are sometimes due to revenge. kill as many enemies as fingers have extended. It is the panagtutuyo practiced by some peasants of Ilocos and other countries. In the Sandwich Islands they amputated a finger to obtain the cure of a serious illness. The same goes for the Hottentots of Africa and the Bushmen. They cut off the little finger to their children, so they don't die. Those from Tonga and Hawaii cut off the phalanges of their fingers and according to Forster, Voyage Around the World. The Guaranis of Paraguay and the Californians cut off their little fingers like ours from their sorrow for the death of a relative. The sacrifice of non-coreligionists was a criminal intrigue of the priests, favored by the caudillos to inflame their own in the war. or in the sense that a person sacrifices himself for others, it will probably have come from the fact that some chief prisoners have managed to escape death by buying their lives with those of their slaves; and if it is with money, it is called a ransom, or bull among the Romanists. According to Grasserie, the sacrifices began as mere offerings to obtain the favors of the gods then as a sign of deference or gratitude; but the "idea of atonement is very late." When men advanced in civilization, they changed human victims with animals, with dolls or with figurines made of clay, paste or flour, as the Romans did and some peoples of India. The former threw the dolls into the Tiber River, and the latter cut off their heads in honor of the gods (Dubois). In Peru the priests said that the gods had abolished human sacrifices. In China they were prohibited in the year 972. Treatise writers understand that the beautiful biblical legend of the suspended sacrifice of Isaac has no other meaning than the abolition of human sacrifices, which Moses had ordered (Lev. XXVII, 28, 29; Numbers, XXV, 4, 5, Deut. XX, 13, 16.) Then it would be another proof anachronism that this legend is after the time of the Hebrew Legislator; The animals sacrificed by Cain were also displeasing to God, and only the fruits offered by Abel were pleasing to God, to which we must add that the prophets continually condemned bloody sacrifices. They are only allowed to eat meat without blood, (that is, those who died a natural death?). Muslims do not make sacrifices nor do Buddhists, and only allow vegetable offerings such as flowers, incense, sandalwood. Strauss says: "The sacrifices with which the barbarian peoples believed to appease divine wrath were originally human. It was a progress when they were changed to animals. The supposed sacrifice of Jesus was a regression.)

CHAPTER 37

SORCERERS

his word means sacrificers, those in charge to offer pigs, hens or other animals to the gods. The Jews had adopted this practice from the Egyptians, and the tiara of the prelates took it from the Assyrians, according to the prophet Ezekiel, (ch. XXIII.) At first, they were the same, but later some were distinguished as healers and visionaries, children of the supernatural spirit of the ancient people. From visionarism and also from charlatanism, sorcerers and fortune-tellers came out of either good or bad faith, if They studied well and really tried to cure the sick with plants, massage, and oils. Although some tribes still lack priests, and only have medical sorcerers, who cure their illnesses, interpret their dreams, and chase away evil spirits; but when their religiosity progresses, when they already know how to pray and offer sacrifices, the sorcerer becomes a priest. Knowledgeable on astronomy, legislation, morals and in general of all elements of science and civilization. The different denominations of the Filipino priests, according to the dialects of each locality, can be categorized as sorcerers, physicians, sacrificers and diviners. We can adopt the classification that Allan Kardec establishes in the Book of Mediums, when he says: "Almost all of us are mediums by nature, but in use only those who have clearly characterized their mediumistic faculty are called that way, which depends more or less on their sensitive organization, and according to their special aptitudes, there are mediums of physical effects, sensitive or impressionable mediums, auditory, speaking, seer, somnambulists, healers, pneumatographers, writers and psychographers. What we know is if the speaking spirits abound more in American

European Spiritism than in the Animism of our mountains, although it is easy to guess that malice is involved and like all things of the civilized, will always be more refined than those of the son of the jungle. Religion arose spontaneously and in good faith from dreams, visions, hallucinations, delusions and mental imbalances or hysteria. The first intermediaries between gods and men were the visionaries, the hysterical, the half-mad or the Guardian's. It is proven that genius and madness have intimate affinities: that the great Guardian's went mad or had moments and traits of madness. Some naturalists believe that genius is nothing more than a mental imbalance; others deny it supposing that they are mere coincidences; but they cannot deny that madness is very common among great Guardian's. The truth is that these visionaries, call themselves auritas (Egypt), magicians (Persia and Chaldea), brahmins or bonsangs (India), prophets (Hebrews), miracle workers (among Romanists), etc. they were the greatest talents that societies had. Even now, among our hill people, if the baglans are highly revered, it is because they are undoubtedly the most intelligent among them. It is not true that they are exploitative rogues. They are the most honorable and virtuous among them, and we can assure you that they act in good faith but hallucinated by the force of the beliefs inherited from our grandparents. Just as in good faith the Romanists believed and still believe in demons and in the efficacy of exorcisms. The Ilocanos still have visionaries who believe they are inspired in dreams by an ancient goddess and are called maibahgbángón. The priests of our mountains are at the same time good healers; They know the miraculous virtues of our medicinal plants. Certain roots, such as the suma (arbutra) and others, which only they know, are effectively antivenoms, just as in pharmacies there are drinks that immunize against poisonous bites. But later, they pretended to know fabulous plants and little stones that serve as amulets and talismans, due to man's inclination to exaggerate his own merits deceiving and exploiting the credulous, no more or less than certain civilized priests, who say things that they themselves do not believe. The Mannilaw pretend to look for the lost objects stolen by means of lights and other ceremonies. The mammadles are diviners. In the Bible we see that in the beginning there were no priests, but each one prayed for himself, the father for his family to the gods, but later the cleverest set themselves up as intermediaries between gods and men, and even priestly castes were formed. These hypocrisies put to priestly rituals and dogmas, true piety and a healthier criterion that are born directly from free reason and conscience. The modern reformers became the prophets of old, Jesus Christ abolished the sacrifices dismissing the temple forever to those who sold little animals for victims, and even before the Lord, they had been condemned by the prophets (Samuel, XV, 22; David, Ps. LI, i6f17; Isaiah, I, 11, 18; Jeremiah, VII, 22 , 23; Amos, V, 22-24; Micah VI, 7, 8; Hosea, VI, 6) whose saying was to remind us of the Sublime Master: "I want mercy and not sacrifice; knowledge of God more than holocausts." Jesus established Apostles, but not Priests. In the Gospels, in the Acts of the Apostles and, it can be assured throughout the New Testament if we eliminate two apocryphal interpolations the name of Priests was only applied to those of the Old Law, but not to the Apostles, elders and deacons of the new. The Philippine Independent Church does well to declare that it has no Priests or Sacrificers, but only Apostles or evangelizing Messengers of Christ.

CHAPTER 38
RITUALS

Temples, rations, symbols, religious dances and myths. The tribes that live in huts, usually bury their corpses in them, or in open places that they mark with stones or burial mounds. These huts or burial mounds gave rise to the temples, as Fergusson demonstrates with respect to India. See what we have said of the dolmens, and of the tombs and temples of the Filipinos. The Indigenous tribes do not pray, simply because of their natural indifference to these abstractions, because they care little about God, and have hardly any ideas of him. Knowing him well enough, they continue to look at him with indifference, and if asked why they do not pray, they reply that the gods do not bother occupying themselves with men, or as the redskins say, to pray is to give lessons to God. But when thunder strikes or danger is imminent, they instinctively seek to disarm the rigor of the gods. his. Symbols are the forms of the ancient religions. According to Pierrot, what was believed to be Egyptian zoolatry was nothing more than a system of symbols by means of animals: the eagle represented Jupiter, as well as the lion Osiris, etc. According to Grasserie, in many cases the deified plants and animals were nothing more than symbols. Sometimes they lead to idolatry, and other times they are traces of it. In Indian and Aryan mythologies, celestial or aerial beings are compared to earth animals, cows are the clouds, the winds are their calves. The stars are also compared with the cows or with the thieves that the sun drives away. The Civilized religions of Paganism are full of symbols, which the Roman Church has inherited. The sacraments are in no way different from the ceremonies to which the Indigenous tribes grant extraordinary virtues.

Those also have their sacraments. The baptism of fire is nothing more than the purification symbolized by fire, according to the Aryans and Hindus. The baptism of water represents the bath to which those who had fallen into captivity underwent to rehabilitate themselves. It is a spiritual purification materialized in the liquid element. Man is very fond of ceremonies, greetings, prostrations, kissing hands or feet, etc. And for this reason, the most ceremonious religions are the most followed, and there is no other remedy than to compromise with their tastes, in order to honestly put them on track in the education of souls. Religious dances. According to some authors, they serve to provoke ecstasy; others suppose that they represent the turns that the sun makes through the zenith. We are of the opinion that just as the Indigenous person believes to conquer the will of his beloved, by singing and dancing, he wants to approach his God by dancing and praising him. David danced in front of the Ark, and the return of the prodigal son was celebrated with dances. Let us therefore have no reason to prohibit decent dances. They were historical enigmas or symbolic stories of gods as if they were men, but which hid religious teachings that the priests explained to the initiates. For example: Jupiter, the father of the gods, engendering Venus, the goddess of beauty, means the Creator who manifests himself to our eyes in the beauty of his works. Saturn devouring his children means Time that devours the days it engenders, or according to Plotinus, the same Creator who continually destroys his own works, or rather, transforms them. Animist religions, according to Grasserie, lack myths and perhaps have reason. But the Filipinos are very fond of the talinhaga (tag.) or enigmatic similarities, to the bugtongs (tag), riddles, or buril (iloc.) They attribute stories to their anthropomorphic gods and legendary characters, but we certainly do not know if they had significance, as in Egypt, India, and Greece. But it is assured that the most popular poem of the Tagalogs, the Life of Laura and Florante, is a series of enigmatic teachings of hidden significance, such as the talinhaga, which are true ingenious myths. The myths of Egypt represented the movements of the Sun or Osiris. Lang in his Mythology he has discovered resemblances between mythological stories and folktales.

CHAPTER 39

DOGMA

Asceticism, Mutilations, Fasts, a Covenant between God and man. ancient Priests, in order to curb the abuses of natural instincts which are fatal to both sexes, invented mutilations at the same time that they prohibited or limited the use of strong drinks, such as the Hindus. The Filipinos practiced circumcision in both sexes to avoid lust, and perhaps also for hygiene in hot countries, according to Renán. Circumcision is a form of material asceticism, common among cultures in Africa, Egypt, the Semites, etc. When the meditations to which the priests indulged had progressed, they fell into very regrettable exaggerations. They tried, nothing less than to annihilate with fasting and martyrdom, the flesh, this life so precious that God had the ineffable generosity to grant us so that we can enjoy it in his peace and grace. with God who is spiritual. It is what they call nirvana. It was imitated by the Essenian Jews and later by the Romanists. "God has no living body here on earth except yours"' said Saint Teresa with admirable eloquence. The spiritualization that we preach does not consist in killing that life, but in thanking the Supreme Benefactor through a pure heart. and works of charity, dispensing with the exclusivist self, but if we have the duty to give bread to our neighbor who needs it, that duty is no less with respect to ourselves. Charity properly understood begins with itself; altruism must be balanced by our obligation to begin to attend to our own needs. Asceticism predisposes to ecstasy and vision. Fasts served to evoke the spirits, that is, with the passage of hunger they became visionaries, because there is nothing like hunger to produce exaltations. But under the guise that by killing the body, man is spiritualized, in reality he is losing his health and reason, contracting serious illnesses. The redskins fast so that they have visions or, as they say and them, so that their gods make revelations to them. And Moses fasted before going up Sinai, as well as Buddha, from whom the supposed fast of Jesus was imitated. What is more certain is that the great Master abolished fasting by saying: "Eat whatever is put before you, because not what enters the mouth contaminates man, but what comes out of it as bad words. The Good Shepherd does not. It is he who kills his sheep, but he who gives them abundant life." And he even added: "I do not say that they withdraw from the world, but only that they beware of evil."(Mark VII, 15-2*; Luke X, 8, and John X, 10; XVII, 15), Pact between God and man Among the Filipinos. In ancient times, when it was seen that a sick person was soon to die, the healthy ones entrusted themselves to him so that he would protect them in the other life, and It seems that this pact was made between them: the anito would protect the living against the evil invisible anitos and other dangers that the spirits can see and foresee, and would do them great favors in exchange for the living serving them meals and others that they would need in the afterlife. In addition, according to the Filipinos, the kibaan, Sankabagway and other anitos of the country, can be enemies or friends through mutual favors and services. See here the origins of the alleged pacts between God and the creature. When man's idea of the relationship between God and his creature was being perfected, he polished those crude beliefs by basing the pact in which man must pay his Creator his homage of gratitude and good works, to deserve Gods protection and his mercy. If we have duties to our heavenly Father, also as his children, we have rights to his loving protection. Therefore, we must always turn to Him with filial trust and unshakable faith in His infinite mercy.

CHAPTER 40
MORALS

Morality in Religion. The child opens his eyes being sensitive; As his reason dawns, he begins to understand and distinguish, preferring what is good; but in his childhood he did not clearly distinguish the good or moral from the bad; he was a cannibal and believed he was doing the right thing. The Vician's killed their parents when they were 40 years old, because as in the other world they will continue to live as in the present, they considered doing well by sending them there in full health, so that they would have greater resistance to cross the long road to Mbulos, abode of souls. Some Indigenous people ate their parents to give them a worthy burial. The Guarani mothers sobbing devoured the corpses of their children in the belief that in this way they would give birth to them again. Morality, then, varies according to the customs and psychology of each people. The morality of the uncivilized, like their knowledge, is embryonic, incomplete and without a fixed direction except towards their selfish conveniences. Morality arose naturally from improvement of the reason, of our noble feelings or that of our own dignity that prevents us from degrading ourselves, and the feeling of justice that forbids us from doing harm to others under penalty of great remorse. Those feelings are perfected when reason enlightens them, and they find educated or good characters who follow their impulses. Morality always progresses and often falls into exaggerations against nature, such as ordering fasts to kill natural instincts and absolute chastity or castration to be equal to God. But everything that is unnatural is impossible and contrary to the will of God, because Nature is the order established by the Lord.

CHAPTER 41
ANTHROPOLOGY OF THE PHILIPPINES

The study of these mythologies and theogony of the various tribes cornered in our Archipelago is useful, because they portray the beliefs of ancient men, and serve to rectify the opinions of the wise men who have tried to scrutinize the origins of Religion. Those men of science already believe in what the Romanists and Protestants say that when man left the kingdoms of God, he knew him because he conversed with him. The historical thing is that even the Bible began to be polytheistic and anthropomorphic. The words of Genesis speak to us of creator gods, Elohim, in the plural, and what Abbé Du-Clot says in Vindicias de la Biblia that all the pages of the Old Testament give this plural form to the name of the God of the Hebrews is inaccurate for Job and Daniel called him Eloha in the singular, because they were really monotheists. Nor is it exact what Bishop Scío asserts that the Hebrews, to honor God, call him in the plural, since they frequently designate him with the names of Adonai (Lord), Yahweh (the Eternal), Shaddai (the Omnipotent) and even of God, Eloha in the singular. And it is much less admissible that the plural alludes to the pagan Trinity, because there is not a single word of such a Trinity in the Old Testament, nor in the New, if the evident neo-Platonic interpolations are eliminated from it, such as it is demonstrated in the Philippine Gospel. And the plural form of Elokim was not accidental: Genesis makes the Gods speak in plural, saying: Let us do (I, 26); One of us (III, 22); Let us descend and confuse (XI, 7). And in vers. 2, 4-8, and 16 of ch. XVIII, which are crudely mixed in a Yahwist document, the divinity is made to appear in three angels or elohim, the compiler having forgotten to fix the resulting contradictions, since as soon as he speaks of a single God as of three elohim. This polytheism is not surprising, since Abraham, Nachor and Laban were polytheists (Josué XXIV, 2; Gen. XXXÍ, 30), that is, the first historical men of the Bible, since almost all of the previous ones were mere symbols of races or peoples. This proves nothing more than the universal law of God on evolution. The Lord endowed us with all the means to perfect our intelligence and our feelings, but he left it to our free will to use them, pointing out as our merit that by our own efforts we seek and find His holy Truth in all things. Thus, religious ideas, like all the others that man harbored in his infancy, began as embryonic, vague, crude, and were perfected until they were elevated and abstract conceptions as that their intelligence developed, as we observe in children and adults. Hume in his History of Religion says: "As far as History reaches, we find the human lineage committed to polytheism. It is unlikely that before the invention of the arts and sciences, there were discoveries. A spiritual monotheism was opened in its Indigenous person state and when it began to civilize, it fell into a gross anthropomorphic polytheism. This would be equivalent to believing that man lived before in palaces than in huts and that he knew Geometry before Agriculture." It may be, Romanists and Protestants will answer scandalized, because then God would have left the first men to live and die like brutes without knowing him. We answer: Yes; They will have lived and died without knowing him well, as right now we see the mountaineers live and die like this in the most remote of our forests, without the Creator condemning anyone for their ignorance. God will have his reasons for acting this way; and we cannot say that he abandons man, from the moment he endowed him with reason, so that with it he investigates the truth. Reason, then, is the true inspiration of the Eternal, and to go systematically against it is to deceive ourselves. The Creator established his law of evolution and according to it, only with continuous progress and development, we will reach truth and perfection. And Hume adds that religion was born from the anxieties of man before the rigors of nature, of his desire to avoid them and to achieve comfort and calm. With these aims he tried to please the beings he feared. Strauss thinks the same and says: "The ancient way, and in a certain natural way, of religion, was polytheism. Man was presented with a plurality of powers that oppressed him and against which he wanted to be protected or from which he wanted to secure himself; a plurality of social relations that he wanted to found and consecrate. He must therefore have thought of a plurality of divine beings. It is confirmed by observation that all the peoples of the earth who are in a certain way in a state of nature, the same today as then, are or were polytheists." The Phoenician Sanconiathon, with temporary 4$ Saul, tried to fix the phases of the development of the Religion through the generations to count from the creation by the line of Cain. The first men considered and adored the vegetables as Gods, although they ate them. Those of this generation were Cain (the first offspring, in Greek Genos) and Cainath (the first daughter, in Greek Genea), they resided in Phoenicia. As they suffered droughts, they raised their arms to the sun (Baal,) asking for mercy as the only Lord of the heavens. Fox (light), Pur (fire) and Phlox (flame) are born, of cane, they drew fire by chance and from them the men learned this» These were: 1. the generation of giants, of which the author of Genesis, VI, also echoes There were cultures of only women, like the legendary amazons. It was when Usous, once saved from the deluge, worshiped fire and wind as gods; he sacrificed animals to them and raised columns that he sprinkled with the blood of those fishes, Halieusr-invents the arts of hunting and of la Chrisor who was Vulcan himself or Tuba-cane, discovered iron and the way to forge it.That is why, after he died , was worshiped as a god with the name of Diamichius. It was carried out in procession in a cart pulled by one or more pairs of oxen. The nomadic tribes form rancherias and dedicate themselves to raising cattle. Two other periods follow in the 1st laasal is discovered, and in the 2nd comes the generation of the cabires and Tot invented the Phoenician alphabet. This is what the Phoenicians believed, because they saw that the uncivilized races performed their cults in the shade of some trees and kept herbs as fetishes that served them as talismans or amulets. And as for the civilized peoples such as Phoenicia, Egypt, Persia, Babylon and India, the cult of the sun was very ancient in them, together with that of fire, which was considered as its image. Also of the Palau Islands, the following was said: "none of these islands is inhabited by only women, which is in the manner of the ancient Amazons, they conserve the species, having trade once a year with the men of a neighboring Island: who each year go to the said Isla, and stop there for some time, and then return to their own; and bolvienda the following year, finding that females have been born from this communication, leaving them. with their mothers in the said Isla, and if they have been born, they take them to their own Islas. Communication from the Jesuit P. Juan Serrano to the King of Spain, 1705. Mr. Retana's archive, Vilano It is an alteration of Tubalcain, Cantú. In India, the cult of the sun was very ancient, united with that of fire, which was considered its image. And without studying the religion of the Indigenous tribes who are the living portrait of ancient man, formed this chronology of religions, which rests on false assumptions. The sages of that time were not yet concerned with Anthropology or Folk-Lore, and surely Sacconiathon could not have presented evidence that Indeed, men began by worshiping plants and successively the sun, giants, fire, wind, and extraordinary men. The ancient Persians told how King Uchenk, meeting a beast in the forest, threw a large stone at it, which was going to stop on a rock, and produced sparks. Uchenk took fire as a divinity and had it worshiped as such by his subjects. The cult of fire is one of the oldest known; but what elevated him to deity was not that mere incident, but the sight of volcanoes and thunderous lightning. The Phoenicians considered it a sacred place or house of God (Beth El), where lightning would explode. Solomon (i), in turn, says that men had for governors the gods of the universe or fire, or to the spirit of the dead, or to the stormy air, or to the turning of the stars, or to the waters, or to the sun and the moon, and even to the useless animals and continues that by idolatry the giants of antiquity perished in the deluge, and it says: "The beginning of religious adulteration was the invention of idols; because they were neither in the beginning nor in the end. Although the Book of Wisdom, because of its Greek or Alexandrian style, is attributed by others to Apollo's, the rival of Saint Paul, or the old Philo, the contemporary of Demetrio. There will always be the vanity of man, it was introduced into the world by them and for that reason, they will soon have an end. Because a father, afflicted by the premature death of his son, made his image and began to honor it as a god the one who was then a dead man and ordered his servants to dedicate ceremonies and sacrifices to him. Thus, an impious custom, becoming stronger in the course of time, became a law, and the images were adored by the tyrants, and those who could not honor them in their presence because they were far away, had the figure of God brought from afar. them, and they honored the image of the king whom they wanted to flatter, as long as he was present. The remarkable ability of the artificer contributed to the superstition of the ignorant, because wanting to please the one who hired him, he put all his art to produce an image with the best perfection. And the multitude of men, seduced by the beauty of the work, to him who a little before was only honored as a man, now worshiped him as a God. Book of Wisdom, XII, 24; XIII, 2; XIV, 12.20. Moreover, this refers to the time of the kings, when man already knew monotheism and had advanced a lot in the Fine Arts. It expresses the origin of idols painted red, but not that of Religion, although Solomon, or whoever wants to be the true author of this book, seems to imply that men, after admiring the beauty of their idols or the virtue and influence of the divinized children, "after knowing so much that they could make a concept of the world: how could they not more easily find the Lord and author of it?" And it excuses in some way the pagans, "for this is what it is said that the Child of his father Bete did, that it says these perhaps err in seeking and desiring to find the true God." XIII, 3-9. Socrates (years 470-400 BC) was already a monotheist, and his contemporary Xenophanes, from Colophon (Greece), the founder of the Eleatic School that produced so many virtuous men, first demonstrated that he cared for the personal gods was a gross idolatry stemming from the deification of men: what his compatriot Evemero expanded and completed in the fourth century before Christ, demonstrating that the gods that were worshiped were not stars nor were they celestial beings, but kings or other famous men who were deified. Aristotle, who was born in the year 384 B.C. said: "The most remote antiquity left to successive centuries under the darkness of fables the beliefs they had of the gods and that the divinity overwhelmed all of Nature. The fable added the rest to force the people to obey the laws for the good of the State. Thus, the gods have come to resemble men, some animals, or other similar things." Metaphysics, book XII, chap. 8. But it is unlikely that such a lofty conception has been capriciously prostituted by the men converting it into crude fetishism. What is clear from Aristotle's words is that fetishism or the fabulous dates from the most remote antiquity and that in his time they already believed that "the gods* had not all the primary natures of all." The opinion of the Epicureans that religion was born of fear is more widely accepted today. Diodorus, who was born in the year 44 B.C., attacked and squeezed by the giants, hid for some time in the form of animals. the gods, in the form of animals, fought commanded by Horus to avenge the death of Osiris; According to Plutarch (year 48 AD) who had a collection of sacred animals, zoolatry originated from the custom of painting figures of animals on flags; but Goguet rightly observes that this cult is prior to the use of flags. Plutarch supposed that the crocodile was adored, because, not having a tongue, it was the symbol of the divinity, who, without speaking, imposed his laws on Nature. But this speculation would have been inaccessible to the crude intelligence of ancient man. The historical thing is that the crocodile was worshiped because it was believed to be the incarnation of the soul of some man, which he had devoured, as the Filipinos believed. Other ancient authors attributed the worship of animals to the Egyptian chiefs who used helmets in the shape of heads. of animals, but peoples who did not wear such helmets also worshiped animals, and it is more probable that, on the contrary, these helmets derived from the cult of animals, perhaps as amulets. Pierret, in Le panthéon égyptien, shows that the Egyptian idols with animal heads were not zoolatry, but mere emblems. Two hundred years ago Voltaire said: "Man began by recognizing only one god, and then the weakness Humanity invented the plurality of gods. A village, or rather, a rancheria, frightened by thunder and lightning, troubled by the loss of the harvest, or evil treated by the neighboring rancheria, knowing its weakness, will have believed that everywhere there is a power superior to us from which good and evil proceeded. It seems impossible to me that at the beginning he thought of the existence of two powers. In everything one begins with the simple, then one arrives at the composite. , and frequently we go back to the simple when we have more knowledge, we answer Precisely in doubtful and conjectural things, many different and vague ideas usually occur at the same time on the same subject until the best study and most careful deep meditation, crystallize our opinion into one." It does not seem likely to me, continues Voltaire, that man began by worshiping the sun or the moon. Children, who are very similar to ignorant men, are not struck by the beauty or usefulness of the sun and the moon, or the variations in their course. They get used to all that without noticing it. We only adore what we fear, and all the children look at heaven with indifference; but when it thunders, they tremble and hide. Undoubtedly ancient men did the same as children. Only later, when a species of philosophers arose who, looking at the course of the stars, discovered their importance, was it when they got men to admire and adore them, but the Indigenous tribes or the simple farmers who were completely ignorant, they did not know enough to adopt a religion that already reveals in advance and to that power that thunders, that spoils our crops and kills our children, to flatter him called Lord: is what the Knef of the Egyptians means; the Adonai of the Syrians, the Baal or Moloch of the Phoenicians, the Bel of the Babylonians, the Papée of the Scythians. Like each small town had its god, from here came the multiplication of gods. Herbert Spencer, in The Cult of Animals, draws the following conclusions: All religion in a rudimentary state is a method to make us propitious to them. deceased ancestors, whom the Indigenous person believes continue to exist in a form no less tangible than the one they had in life, with the power to do good or harm to the living. These sentiments and ideas that he has with respect to said deceased constitute the entire foundation of his superstitions. Indigenous tribes have the custom of giving themselves nicknames after animals or plants, and furthermore, according to the testimony of Dr. Miligan, they take their names from objects, events or acts of nature. From here the misunderstanding was born, very easy to commit due to the scarcity of words and means of transmission in the Indigenous tribes. and if their name was ox or lion, they would believe they were children of an ox, like the worshipers of the ox (Hindus, Egyptians or of the lion (Assyrians, Romans, etc.) "Each tribe considers itself descended from the being that is the object of their adoration*Only in this way would the legends that originally animals spoke, stole women, collected and educated children, etc., when tradition preserves the memory of two branches of ancestors under different names, of the pure Tagalog's and to the Apo of the

Ilocanos and other Filipino hedges. All animals, the fruit of this crossing will be represented with the body of one of those animals and the head of the other, like the Pacht goddess of Egypt who has the form of a woman with the head of a lion, or the winged lions of Babylon. one of the reasons why abstract and collective names have taken on an anthropomorphic sense. This is why the cult of purely anthropomorphic divinities comes later, when the language is sufficiently formed so that the distinction between true names and nicknames can be preserved in the new tradition. What most justifies this theory, or better shows its accuracy, is that it is in accordance with the general law of evolution: from a simple ancient belief, vague in its form, it gives birth to our eyes, by continual differentiations, the numerous and heterogeneous forms of beliefs that have existed and exist. The desire to have the second self (soul) of the dead ascendant propitious, a common desire between the Indigenous person and the civilized, has been everywhere the first form of religion: hence he concludes Spencer the numerous and different forms just cited have come into being." Fustel de Coulanges and Grasserie are also of the opinion that religion arose from ancestor worship. Sir John Lubbock, in Origins of Civilization, attempts to show that animals, plants, water, mountains, stones, fire, heavenly bodies, and a multitude of other objects, are and have been worshiped very extensively and sometimes simultaneously, so that they cannot serve as a basis for a natural classification of religions, and he enumerates as the great stages of the development of the religious idea, the following: 1) Atheism: Not the denial of the existence of a God, but the lack of defined ideas In religion among the wildest, According to him, this stage is represented, among others, by the Australians, who only have some vague ideas about the existence of a spiteful and malevolent being, but weak and fearful only in the dark, and the general fear of the curse. They have no idea of creation, prayers, or religious ceremonies; everything that constitutes the cult is unknown to them. They do not believe in the existence of a God; nor do they have words to express God and soul like the Indians of California, if we believe Father Baegert, who says he lived with them seventeen years. It is asserted that certain Eskimo* tribes have no religion either, the Polynesians (Palaos), the Indians of the Sacramento and San Joaquin Valleys (Brazil), nor the Kaffirs, Hottentots and other South Africans.[23] However, Lubbock confesses that they do not stop believing in invisible beings; and even if he doesn't want it, without a doubt that is an embryonic Religion. 2) Until now it has been defined as the cult of material things, confusing it with idolatry. But the idol is an object of worship, while the fetish places the divinity under the power of man. The Indigenous person does not worship his fetish but uses it to dominate and counteract the spirit or divinity he represents, forcing him to fulfill his desires, not by virtue of the offerings, food, and sometimes with human sacrifices accompanied by dances. Many times, they insult their divinity and beat him to force him to be good or to grant what they want. In substance, fetishism is pure curse. Sorcerers of all the world think that by obtaining something from the enemy (such as hair, scraps of clothing, portrait, etc.), they achieve a certain power over him. A simple piece of his clothing is enough for this, and when not, it seems to them that any damage caused to their image will affect the original. They attribute death to the curse of some enemy, so they avenge it on the suspect. subject to the same passions as man. There are tribes that do not know a benevolent god like the Veddas of Sri Lanka. Such gods are won with food and not with prayer; they are not creators, omniscient, or all-powerful. They are less material than us, but like us mortals, and that if they are more powerful than man in certain respects, in others they are less so. In their religion, if it can be called that, morality does not enter at all. The words good or bad refer to the sense of taste or material well-being, and not to the idea of right or wrong. These gods neither reward good nor punish evil, but often approve of it, not virtue.[24] Fetishism lacks temples, idols, priests, sacrifices and prayers, except in rare cases. This is religion in a tiny phase, reduced to the simple belief in evil beings; but the Mountain Tribe's nor do they have a demon in their essential character as tempter. Lubbock's added fetishism is commonly applied to Negritos, but it is actually recorded everywhere. The world. 3) Totemism: It is the worship of natural objects and beings, such as trees, lakes, rivers, stars, stones, mountains animals, the lingam or phallus etc. Lubbock believes with Spencer that this cult came from the names or nicknames of animals that were given to the ancestors, and that is why it is called Totemism. This word comes from North America. The god, patron or coat of arms of each tribe or family is called a totem. According to Schoolcraft, the redskins trace their genealogy back to the animal that serves as their totem. In South Africa, the Bechuana tribes are divided into men of the monkey, the lion, the crocodile, the elephant, the ox, the porcupine, etc., and no one eats the meat of their respective totem. The curse, says Lubbock, it no longer defeats the gods; but they are still not considered supernatural creators, but rather parts of nature; they are superhuman, species, not individuals. The spirits no longer die as quickly as the body; they make long journeys, and their grandparents die out along the way. Heaven is a distant part of the earth. The cult of the stars, he says, in its ancient form did not differ essentially from the cult of a mountain or a river. 4) Shamanism: The cult of these Magicians is what they call "Shamanism". Hitherto the divinities were viable; but now they already acquire the character of spirits, although sometimes they allow themselves to be seen; they are already much more powerful than man and come to be considered as a different nature; rather than spirits. of the deceased* they become true deities or Guardian's. Their dwelling is also very far away and is only accessible to shamans. and so, they pretend to be inspired by the genius in whose name they speak and pronounce oracles. taught or transmitted from one to another; although it is so widespread, it seems to be born in each individual separately as the fruit of an imagination superseded under the influence of very similar impressions, throughout all the deserts of the north of Mexico and Siberia. 5) idolatry or anthropomorphism: In this phase, according to Lubbock, the gods take on a more fully human nature, but remain more powerful. They can still be reduced by persuasion; mm part of nature, and not creators of it. They are represented by images or idols. The cited author believes that the monarchy existed before idolatry, and says: "In the lowest religions, the Indigenous person adores objects without having a definite idea of divinity. But when the region acquires a character more intellectual, when he embraces faith as well as dissent, belief as well as mystery, Man conceives divinity for the first time as a being similar to him in form, character and attributes, even more wise and powerful. It is one of the reasons why the gods are anthropomorphic in this phase." 6) Supernaturalism: In this phase, according to Lubbock, divinity is seen as the author of nature, and not as a simple part of it. For the first time he becomes a truly supernatural being. Little by little the spirit of man was elevated, thanks to a better understanding of natural laws. He began by supposing that the divinity had formed the earth, taking it out of the waters, and preparing it for the mansion of humanity; and then he conceived the idea that earth and water had been created alike by supernatural power. After having regarded all spirits as malefic, he elevated himself to the belief in good divinities as well as in evil divinities; and gradually subordinating the latter to the former, he adored as gods only the good spirits, descending the bad ones to the condition of demons. and last phase: Moral religion. From simple belief, Lubbock says, in the manes, he came step by step to the recognition of the soul; Finally, uniting this belief with that of a just and beneficent being, he associated morality with religion. The sacred character that today forms an integral part of our conception of duty could not arise until religion became moral; and the latter could not be verified until the divinities were conceived as benefactors, who rewarded good acts and punished bad ones. This step was an immense progress for humanity, since the fear of the invisible powers, whose influence had only been used to produce simple ceremonies and sacrifices, immediately endowed moral sentiments with a sacred character, and, for the same reason, of a force that until then they had not had. This is in short, the famous theory of Sir John Lubbock, based on mere references by other authors, not always exact. We who have lived close to diverse mountain races of the Philippines and even believed their own superstitions in our childhood, for which we know in depth what he calls shamanism, and the cults of animals, stars, mountains, anitos etc., we find ourselves able to rectify some errors of his own and of others. In the first place, although we accept that man must have begun by not looking at or believing in God or any religion in his early childhood, this state of complete atheism must not have lasted much longer than the first death or the outbreak of the first storm that he has witnessed. Gabriel de Mortillet and other prehistorians maintain that man from the Neolithic period was religious because of his way of burying the dead and because of the amulets that he wore. They were found next to the corpses. There were skulls marked with a T. In a bronze age grave found in Kivik (Belle Island) there were sun emblems. There is also a figure of the sun on a column from the Iron Age discovered in Italy, photographs of which are found in the Philippine Bible. I do not believe that there is any race today that does not have its religion more or less embryonic or cultured. What happens is that the Indigenous tribes do not want to communicate their religious ideas to strangers as it may desecrate their beliefs, and it is only with great difficulty that they reveal anything to us and the Europeans, much less. For this reason, strange travelers usually say that this or that tribe lacks religion, because that is how, in effect, they assure it, as our mountaineers usually do. The well-informed Fray Ferrando and the scholar Peñarrubia, who was Governor of Abra several times, assured that the Mountain Tribe's of that province lack religion, and this error was believed among the Spaniards. What Father Baegert says of the Indians from California who lack the words to express the ideas of God and soul, so the missionaries kept the Castilian voices, the same thing happened in our Archipelago, not for lack of Filipino voices; but because of the inquisitorial and intransigent rigor with which the friars prohibited the use of names that recall the ancient ancestors of the Filipinos until the civilized have completely forgotten them. In Ilocos, the authorities of the Roman Church, which was the only prevailing, exclusive and tyrannical, prohibited the use of the Ilocano word buniag to express the verb to baptize, using instead the Castilian baptizar for not remembering Kabunían, god of the Igorot's, At the Synod of Kalasiaw (Pangasinan) held by Bishop Garcia in 1773, we also do not accept that the Indigenous tribes do not believe in another life. Lubbock's error that there are races without religion has already been refuted by eminent ethnographers. and by the Vienna theologian Gustavo Roskoff in his Religion among the wild peoples. Cicero once said: "Therefore among all the varieties of living beings, there is no creature except man which has any knowledge of God, and among men themselves, there is no race either so highly civilized or so savage as not to know that it must believe in a god, even if it does not know in what sort of god it ought to believe. Thus, it is clear that man recognizes God because, in a way, he remembers and recognizes the source from which he sprang." Lubbock himself affirms: "If the mere feeling of fear and the idea that there are probably other Beings more powerful than us, are enough to constitute a religion, so I think we should consider that all mankind has a religion, but it is never taken as proof of religiosity that the child is afraid of darkness and recoils before a dark room. In this case we could say that the horse and the dog recognize their master as

God for fearing and venerating him. The dog barks at the moon. "Yes; that is the rudiment of religion, even among animals, as Darwin shows in The Descent of Man; and if not, what would we call it? It seems that Lubbock does not express well what he calls Fetishism. According to his explanations, he wanted to refer to the belief in talismans, which is truly typical of the mountain tribes; but those are not deities but prodigious means. And then the amalgamation with witchcraft that is already of the civilized of the Middle Ages. Until now it is believed in Spain, in other parts of Europe, and among the peasants of the Philippines, that witches or meigas can harm people by means of their hair, clothes, portraits or just by pricking a doll with pins in the part that it is desired that they suffer. In Spain, even now, the peasants bathe, put in wells, burn or hit certain images of saints when they want to force them to grant them rain or other things they want. In Visayas it is called holom to submerge idols or images of Saints in water during droughts until it rains. The Mandaya's of Mindanao beat the idols of their evil Guardian's. Despite what Lubbock says, the fetish is the same idol, the same one that the Indigenous person and the peasant worship or punish, according to the degree of development of his intelligence. Nor is it exact that all the gods of the Indigenous person are bad: good is the protective ancestor of each tribe; and bad or enemy is the god of the enemy tribe, and to him they attribute all their children, illnesses until death, for which they take revenge on the people of the enemies, like the panagtutuyo of the Ilocano and other mountain tribes. For me, the first phase of Religion in its origins had as its background the belief in reincarnation, as I have shown, and hence the cult of fetishes or beings of nature, in which the races suppose the souls of dead souls become incarnated. What I will call Totemism Schoolcraft, Lubboc and others, is very different from how we know it directly. Perhaps the panthropic madness that consists in believing oneself transformed into an animal and is contributed to zoolatry.

very common among all the races of the world. Regarding Shamanism, Lubbock confesses that it is difficult to distinguish it from Totemism and Idolatry practiced in the Visayas islands at the time of the Spanish Conquest, according to a communication to the King from Governor Legazpi before arriving in Manila; we saw the Tinguians of Abra and the farmers of Ilocos practice it. It happens when the belief in the Anitos or souls of the ancestors comes to have idols, temples and priests who are at the same time healers, diviners and sorcerers. Nor are we satisfied that anthropomorphism is the same as idolatry, for one can be an anthropomorphist, without being an idolater, like the Protestants and Jews who adopt the anthropomorphism of the Bible, and yet abhor images. Nor do we find it acceptable that the religion that attributes God human forms, be separated from Anitism, the same that serves as the background to Totemism and Shamanism. If the mountain races believe that their deities are the half-material, half-spiritual souls of their ancestors, close or remote? Being sometimes visible, how strange is it that they attribute human forms to them and make images of them? Grasserie, in his Psychology of Religions, thinks like the ancient Epicureans and says: "Fear was certainly the beginning of Religion. Out of fear, man submitted to the natural forces, which were superior to him. Some of these forces seemed favorable to him, others hostile; he asked for help from the religion was at first subjective, that is, man worshiped his own ancestors, then the dead in general, sometimes the living, finally the saint and the demigod. The religion in its origins was the cult of the dead and domestic. Later she became objective and worshiped all things in nature. He began to believe as many gods as there were anthropomorphized spirits in nature. Then a hierarchy of these gods was made: the sun, for example, brighter and higher, must have been superior to the divinized spring or tree. the gods were classified as superior and inferior, naturally these were relegated to oblivion, ending up with only the one who prevailed in opinion remaining. Fatally, therefore, monotheism was born from polytheism. Theogonies indicate that they have come, not from a single religion, but from the same father or criterion, which is the human Spirit. The polytheistic and anthropomorphic religion forms its mythology, and when it progresses it becomes monotheistic, establishes dogmas and forms its theology. Religion has three parts: dogma or myth, morality, and worship. It has begun with worship; religion has been practiced before knowing it well. Religions have lived long you time without morality: morality was entirely separated from religion: man, only asked the gods for health, happiness, security, and victories. The Adam and Eve themselves were not yet entrusted with practicing good and avoiding evil, but only obeying a ritual precept: the prohibition of eating the fruit was purely ritual, because it was not bad in itself, but as an infraction of a divine mandate, like among the Greeks the prohibition to open Pandora's box-- With their disobedience they discovered natural morality. of these progresses it joins religion, which in its turn will have already become spiritualized. The action of morality has contributed to the progress of monotheism. "The egoistic motives he adds are mainly due to fear; the mixed ones to interest; and the altruistic ones to love. The preservation instinct has created the belief in the immortality of the soul; that of fear has given rise to demonic religion; and that of happiness, religion proper. The sight of present inequalities and the psychological instinct of justice have corroborated the belief in the immortality of the soul. soul and in future rewards and punishments, and then the religion of justice was born. with their riches. All are equal, nobody is happier, except insofar as it is better; nor more unfortunate, but insofar as it is worse. After the feeling of love, the religion of charity is born, of self-denial and asceticism or desire to identify with a God, spiritualizing one or stripping oneself of their own personality: it is the nirvana of the Buddhists, the communion of Catholics with God. Having seen the various opinions of the wise, let us hear what the mountaineers themselves say. An intelligent Negro explained to Bosman how they make and unmake gods, saying : "When we undertake something important, we look for a god, who favors our company, and going out, we take for God the first thing that is presented to us: a dog, a cat, a stone, a piece of wood or another object. To that god we present an offering, solemnly swearing that if it favors our desires, we shall henceforth adore it and esteem it as a god. If our undertaking succeeds, we have already discovered a new and useful god, to whom we make daily offerings; but if not, that God is thrown away like a useless instrument. Thus, we make and unmake gods every day, consequently we are the masters and the inventors of what we adore. They paint; then, a few meters from their cabins, they clean the land of weeds in a space of half a meter; they place the stone there and worship it as a god, offering it tobacco and feathers, and begging it to deliver them from dangers and what difference is there between these Indigenous tribes and the Romanist who makes a more or less artistic sculpture out of a piece of wood or ivory and then idolizes it like a god . Such news, without being deepened, have led Grasserie and other authors to believe that in the period of fetishism, when the idea of divine revelation has not yet begun, the Indigenous person invents his god, which is inaccurate. The Indigenous person believes that through certain ceremonies performed by his priests, their invisible god or gods incarnate in the stones that have some resemblance to men, or in the "animals, in which they believe they usually incarnate; but they can be wrong. When the company fails, it is a sign that the chosen animal was an ordinary one, and not the incarnation of a god or of a deified soul and for that reason they leave him and even beat him out of disappointment. But it is unlikely that the Indigenous person adores the animal or any stone, if he does not believe in good faith that within them is divinity, like the Romanist who innocently worships the idols of the Saints. The Tinguians of Abra worship a pile of small stones and other large ones half a yard long and a quarter wide that are in the shape of a man. When a wealthy person becomes seriously ill, on the advice of the baglan (priest) they prepare food, get drunk and make a great uproar, and brandishing their spears, they go to the outskirts of the settlement where the stone is found. There the baglan sacrifices a rooster or pig to him, spilling the blood on the head of the idol. With this ceremony the stone is consecrated. And he becomes Anito, just like the host when the Catholic Priest pronounces the magic word over the wafer: The Malays distinguish alligators and crocodiles as divine. Hoc Est corpus Meum (this is my body), when said becomes a real spell. Then, they dress and season the victim by also cooking rice, and then the baglan offers the food with prayers to the new idol. The Anito invisibly consumes the substance of the offerings. When the baglan declares that Anito has finished eating, those present consume the offerings in the belief that they are taking bland and insubstantial food. it is completely correct that the Indigenous tribes invent their gods just like that.

CHAPTER 42

THE REBIRTH

ummarizing, Without pretending to fix the success of the phases of Religion, which is exposed to errors, we deduce the following conclusions:

1) Unconsciousness: The ancient man in his state of unconsciousness was not concerned with attributing to a god or gods the causes of the wonders and phenomena of the Universe, supposing that they were natural or spontaneous.

2) Fear of phenomenon: no matter how indifferent, the rumble of thunder, the imposing aspect of the volcanoes and the seas in revolution, the impetus of the hurricanes, the presence of the beasts did not fail to amaze me. That destroyed the men who came within their reach and above all, the spectacle of an agony and the death of a relative. This dread, this fear of mysterious forces, superior to those of man, was the determining cause of the religious idea. This fear was instinctive, and could not yet be called religion, because he was still unable to relate those phenomena except that he feared the existence of gods or animated forces superior to him. I still didn't think about souls or spirits.

3) Anitism: When his reason was cleared up, the death of his loved ones could not help but deeply wound his feelings, nor impress and make him ponder his own shadow and the appearance of his portrait in the mirror of the waters. Relating both phenomena to his dreams and certain strange noises, he thought of a half-spirit that survives man when he dies. It is what the Filipinos and Malays call anito, and the Latins

call it anima, from the same root ani, (soul) The spirit, that imponderable force that gives life to the body, really exists as electricity and ether exist, equally imponderable forces, which they only manifest themselves in their effects. The newly dead body is entirely the same as when it was still alive, and yet it no longer lives, because it has no spirit. Therefore, the existence of the agent called spirit or soul is as real as life. And the soul is immortal, because if it is a spirit, it does not have a corruptible body; and if it is simply energy, such as ether, gas, electricity, psyche, plasma, or whatever you like, it does not die either by the physical law of conservation of energy or of substance. I believe that the human seed, coming out of its father, already carries its soul germ, as if it already has life and movement, seen through a microscope. The souls, then, that animate the new beings, are offspring of the parent souls, as if they preserve the Guardians of their parents, and sometimes of their mothers. We are almost satisfied with the Bible, that is, that the soul can almost be identified with life, although we do not know its true nature. We know that it is an imponderable energy, but we do not know if it is absolutely spirit-mind, or if spirit can exist without matter.

4) Reincarnation Fetishism and Anthropomorphism: Then ancient man began inquiring where this spirit should go after the death of the body, thought that the spirits of those devoured by beasts, amphibians, cetaceans and even by lightning, would reincarnate in them; those of the drowned would remain in the waters like little angels or genies; and those buried in houses, forests and caves, would continue in them as domestic anitos, from forests and caves. Therefore, ancient fetishism embraces, without being able to establish a succession of phases, phenomenology, zoolatry, phytolatry and other cults. Religion was born from the deification of hunger, and Anthropomorphism was its natural and immediate manifestation. souls of the good ones would go to enjoy an earthly Paradise on the top of the highest and most remote mountains, and those of the bad ones would reincarnate in

animals to see if they could improve it, they would end up harming the living. The sinister and absurd idea of hell after death could never occur to the angelic feelings of the child-man.

5) Gods of space: The phenomenon of mirage that make us see men in space, made us think that those spirits also come to populate the air and are called katatawan, Sankabagway, etc. in the Philippines, and among the other peoples, Indra god of the air etc. And since these mirages portray complete panoramas with their plants and animals, and also because these beings also have shadows, it was assumed that they would pass to another vine and that this one is similar to the present one.

6) Euhemerism or Deification of Kings: Applies the name of Elokim indistinctly to the gods and to the kings or judges, as the first ones were called The Bible rulers of the tribes of Israel From remote antiquity, euhemerism demonstrated that all the gods of the ancient civilized peoples had been kings, as happened in the Philippines and among the uncivil peoples. "There can hardly be any doubt," says Hale in his Ethnography of the United States, "that the divinities worshiped in the southern groups of Micronesia were nothing but deified chiefs, whose existence has faded from memory with time. I believe they made the souls of the kings as kings of souls, that is, gods.

7) Giants and statues: The remains of the gigantic prehistoric animals and trees, made us think of the existence of gigantic men, supposing that those that by mere coincidence seem to be human footprints imprinted on certain mountains and rocks were theirs.[25] So they assumed that our ancestors were giants, and that they were able to build the dome of heaven.

8)Transmigration and Sabianism: When the Chinese, the Indians, the Egyptian Aurites, the magicians Chaldeans, and other priests had occupied themselves in studying the stars and understood their true importance, it was thought of the transmigration of extraordinary souls making them climb through the rainbow as a bridge, the souls of their kings, legislators and heroes. The first form of Sabianism grew out of this belief. The priests and kings had ascended and identified themselves with the Sun, the Moon, Sirius, the brightest star, and the planets. Mirages will have opened the way to this supposition.

9) The Rainbow: Then, which at the time, of ancient anthropomorphism, was nothing more than the belt or loincloth of the greatest deified Anito, in Persia became the Chinevad bridge between heaven and earth, or in a celestial ladder as Jacob and the Germans believed, and an author says that even the Malays and Polynesians believed. The rainbow, then, becomes the sign of the promise of a better life for the good. This is the rational origin of the scientific absurdity of the rainbow as a sign of alliance between God and Noah, and we say absurd, because as before that fact, there had been rains, it is impossible that the rainbow had not also existed before, which is the effect of the refraction of the sun's rays in the rain.

10) Idolatry: Emerged from the moment that man knew how to roughly carve the images of his anthropomorphic gods. The idols of today's ancient peoples and mountain people have human forms.

11) Polytheism: It was born from the time of fetishism, as many were the deceased, the beings and objects in which those believed to reincarnate. Another polytheism was derived from the mixture of peoples, and for political purposes the gods of the various allied peoples were brought together in a single pantheon.

12) Bad and Good Gods: Certain tribes of the ancient man were not concerned with making their gods good; they believed them to be like them with their virtues and defects, that is, with

their alternatives of good and bad. They did not distinguish the gods, the Melanesians, those of New Zealand and Dahomey also worshiped him. These qualities: but later, as among the deceased there were good and bad, friends and enemies, they attributed their misfortunes to the bad or to the enemies and implored the protection of the good against them. Thus arose the division of the gods into bad and good.

13) Dualism: The ancient division of the gods? "Good and bad" things gradually acquired new forms: first astronomical and later metaphysical of the From the beginning man was horrified by the sight charity for unforeseen mishaps that should have found in her, just as he always experienced joy with the appearance of light, he therefore attached himself to the light as a benevolent goddess, already in the sun, already in the fire, its image of him"; and unto darkness as an evil god. Here we have the dualism in embryo that also took shape the belief that the eclipse is the fight between' the Sun and the serpent in the form of a cloud, represented in Ormuzd and Ahriman, gods of two antagonistic peoples, the Iran and the Turan, also took shape, and it is recorded that almost all the gods who thought they were evil or demons, were those of the towns enemies peoples, and for these, vice versa (Parsi, Hindu and Chinese periods).This dualism was later spiritualized by Zoroaster between the struggle of good and evil, between God and the Devil. When man was moralizing, he gave preference to the good gods until he raised the good gods from the oceans, and the bad ones he threw into Ondera, Amenti or into the imaginary Hell. And just as the concept of God rises with continuous progress, and becoming increasingly important, the absurd existence of the devil is being annulled and denied. The educated people of Europe no longer believe that evil exists. Bad thoughts, bad inclinations and vices, are exclusively our indignities or rudeness of the matter, but exclusively ours and not of any invisible devil.

14) Trinities: Certainly, we do not know if they were prior to

Dualism, or if they were born from it. According to the Code of Manu, IX, 45, "the complete man is made up of himself, his wife and his child." All the ancient gods had their respective wives, and consequently daughters or sons. Was the ancient idea of the Trinity born from here? Thus, we have seen it in Osiris, Isis and Horus of Egypt; Belo, Semiramis and the Child of Babylon;[26] Brahma, Saravadi and Vishnu. But perhaps they were also formed with the alliance of various peoples, uniting their respective gods and relegating those of the less influential peoples to second order.

15) God and the goddesses: When humanity, with the astronomical progress of the Chinese, Chaldeans, and Egyptians, came to know the universal influence of the Sun on the earth and the entire planetary system of which it is the center, then it was worshiped as the Highest God. (the Elium of the Phoenicians) and the planets as their ministers or secondary gods (Phoenicians, Chaldeans, etc.)

16) Monotheism And following the law of selection: the Sun ended up remaining alone, realizing that he who did as many wonders as the Universe contains, could do so with only his omnipotent will or word without the need of secondary gods called elohim, beautiful-planets, Anachspands (seven great ones) or angels."The great All, as Voltaire says, must have had only one Great Spirit.

17) Holy Ghost: Mankind always progressing in the sciences, discovered that the Sun , with being prodigiously immense and the true life of how many beings surround it, it was not more than one of the innumerable planetary centers. Then he glimpsed the astonishing immensity of the Universe and the infinite greatness of its Maker; then he understood that, if Well, all the magnificent works of God participate in his ineffable perfection and beauty, yet there is none of those creatures worthy of representing him due to the impossibility of any of

the parts giving a full idea of the harmonious whole or of its author. The man came to imagine that God is a Spirit, forbidding making images of any creature or thing that is in the sky, on earth or in the water (Exodus XX, 4).

18) Religion and Morality: Those who had begun as simple seers, hysterics, hallucinations, or tricksters, sorcerers, and fortune-tellers, gradually perfected themselves as priests, astronomers, physicians, philosophers, and sociologists, and took advantage of the faith of the people in their oracles. to establish social and moral rules in the name of God. Just as Religion was born from fear, priests took advantage of it to moralize societies. When Morality was associated with Religion, it elevated it and contributed to monotheism, separating from the other gods and placing the ideal God of goodness at the top of the heavens; but he exaggerated by inventing penalties for the afterlife that were previously "unknown," according to Grasserie. Religion and Morals complete each other; the first gives divine sanction to the precepts of Morals, and Religion rises in the eyes of believers by appearing as the Teacher of the purest morality, and like Morality, Religion began with the sensible, continued with the most rational, and will end up eliminating all that is absurd and unnatural, remaining with the real and positive good.

19) God is not an invention of fantasy: God was not a mere invention of man's fantasy, but a thing the most necessary of all that we can conceive, whose existence first divined his instinct and then they confirmed his observations, his mature reason and the progress of his admirable science. God is as real and obvious as the Universe, and it follows that his work is as real and obvious to our eyes. Only his infinite omnipotence and wisdom could do it, and only his ineffable and sweetest love of Father can keep it. The most atheistic men of science get to know the second causes in their studies and analyses, but they know and confess that there is another unknowable first cause, which for not calling it God, they designate it with the

names of "blind Chance" or "spontaneous nature", as if chance with its acknowledged blindness, and an incognito being like nature, could work as many marvels as the various beings and organisms contain, which show the supreme wisdom of their Creator, In this they go back to the crude idea of races in an ancient or Indigenous person state, which attribute everything to unconscious Nature. But God exists, as the first cause must necessarily exist, the agent and the preserver of everything there is, of everything that moves, of all life and of all death, or rather, of all transformation. He is a Being above all consideration, His divine nature is perhaps inaccessible to the very limited intelligence of man; but we guess it; we clearly see his existence, his power and his wisdom in his portentous works, we hear his most holy voice in the depths of our conscience; we experience the sweetness of his loving and diligent paternity in the providential satisfaction of our daily needs.

20) God and Nature: Let us define before, because many times what atheists call Nature, is the same that we designate with the name of God. For some, Nature is the imponderable Supreme Agent (such as the ether, electricity, etc.) that gives life and directs everything that exists in the Universe. Under this concept, it is the same that we call God, since we do not pay attention to the insignificant difference in appreciation of whether God is Spirit or nature like electricity or gas (no one really knows); but in the existence of an intelligent and conscious Being, who directs everything with marvelous wisdom. This is accurate; and what we do not accept is that in Nature there is a spontaneous and unconscious agent.

21) Pantheism: Now, in the acceptance of Nature as the Universe, the Pantheists say that God is the Universe, Büchner demonstrates that there is no force without matter, nor matter without force. Thus, God, who is the Supreme Force or Energy, could not exist without matter on which to act, From which it

follows that God coexists with Matter, being eternal Matter like God, Corollary: We are parts of the Divinity: our body is part of matter, and our spirit is part of the great Spirit, God, But we object: God being omnipotent, wise, good, pure and holy, as we see him in his magnificent works, he must have begun with making himself the most perfect. Like all existing matter in the Universe, although they are perfectible, they are not yet perfect. More clearly, how can we claim to be part of Divinity with all our great defects, sometimes impurities and sometimes crimes? Can the Divinity be identified with a corrupted being or object? No. Therefore, God cannot be the Universe.

22) Agent, Verb and Object: Let's be specific; according to me in my humble opinion, there is an incredible Intelligence that produces and directs everything wisely, and that Intelligence is at the same time the Supreme Goodness, judging by six providential and inexhaustible mercies. This Being sublime is what we call God, And Nature is the law of God printed to the Universe, thus they exist: God, as Agent, Nature as Verb or Law, and the Universe as Object.

23) Religion: Being God is an intelligent and conscious Being, and since we, his creatures, are intelligent and conscious, it is logical to suppose that He endowed us with intelligence, conscience and feelings, so that with our intelligence we seek him and know him in the only path of truth that is science; so that with our conscience we always act justly, following the holy laws that are naturally imprinted onto our heart; and so that with our feelings we know how to adore and thank our Sublime Benefactor, and love our brothers, the other creatures. In a word, God likes to have direct communication with us intellectually, sentimentally or cordially; but not with lies from deceitful intermediaries. oh! It is undeniable that our intelligence and our hearts instinctively seek our most loving error. If we want them to respect our beliefs, we begin by demonstrating our exquisite education in the deep respect for others.

THE END

This book was created in the workshops of The Philippines Rebirth on the 19th of November 1909.

FOOTNOTES:

[1] The Tagalogists noticed that the Igorot's had already the pronunciations of the n with tilde, gu, ak, and, f.

[2] SPIRITISM IS PRESTIDIGITATION: How strange it is that the poor Filipino mountaineers entertain these ancient beliefs, if even the modern spiritualists in the guise of scientists, follow identical practices? The medium, by evoking the Spirit, gets hard

and when he speaks, he makes believe that whoever does it it is the Spirit, and it also blows wind from the dark room. In the same way, the God of Genesis (III, 8) walked in Eden whistling on the wings of the wind, and The Bible speaks of visionaries and the like. The Spanish chroniclers of the XVI, XVII and XVIII centuries, almost all friars who hated and persecuted to death with its barbarous Tribunal of the Inquisition, to all religion that was not its own, and to superstitions; They unanimously assure that the baglans were in communication with invisible beings and that they made accurate predictions. This proves nothing more than by dint of ancient beliefs, however erroneous they may be, because they take root in consciences as of second nature science as second nature. Grasserie says: "When religious belief almost disappears from a country; when the Christian religion (of Catholics and Protestants) is almost excommunicated from civil societies, the piety that remains towards the dead is surprising and that it intensifies when the immortality is doubted. of the soul, which is contradictory Almost all contemporary spirits admit reincarnation in the centuries of incredulity, the religion of the dead has survived religion properly happiness." After having attended several seances in Barcelona, I do not believe in his scientificism, because everything hidden inspires mistrust, and of course what is not wanted or can not be demonstrated cannot be scientific. If there were something true in the phenomena produced by the spiritualists, it would be known and sanctioned by science; but the truth is that they cannot act except in the dim light, surrounded by people who are their friends and in their own homes. The English Courts have just ruled in favor of the conjurer Mashenyo who bet a thousand dollars against the spiritualist Corney, promising to produce and did produce by means of conjuring the apparitions and other phenomena that the spiritualists attributed to spirits. In the controversy that these days was established in the Columns of the French newspaper Le-Matin, the wise Gustavo Le Bon offered a prize of five hundred francs to the spiritualist who lifted an object without touching it, which is the a b c of Spiritism, according to Morselli; but that it be photographed with a snapshot, because when they photographed objects that a fakir from India made appear and disappear from public view, it was discovered that the objects apparently disappeared by an optical illusion, remained in their places, as the photograph demonstrated The spiritualists excused themselves with the idea that the spirits do not want to act except in semi-obscurity. And in this, too, Le Bon caught them in a waiver, since they publish in their magazines so-called photographs made in the vivid and dazzling light of magnesium. In Barcelona, to convince the public, the spiritualist's there have published some photographs of spirits that have appeared to certain Filipino mediums, whom I saw tease the credulous. To the main one I sold some books that deal with these photographs so that he could refine his jokes a bit* But the spiritualists over there believe the photographs taken in Manila out of hand. And vice versa, the spiritualists of the Philippines will believe in the pretended apparitions described in the two spiritualist newspapers of Catalonia. And roll the ball, which over long distances, long lies too. The medium Mr. Jacinto Fornaguera, Director of La Razón Espiritista de Barcelona, whom I asked; why even the men of science have not sanctioned Spiritism, he answered me: They believe in Spiritism; but they do not confess it publicly for fear of ridicule. When these days the director of Fabra Observatory Mr. Comas Sola scientifically unmasked the spiritualist's -of Barcelona in the magazine La Actualidad, they did not find a newspaper that wanted to continue publishing their defense for fear of that ridicule, as Fornaguera confesses in his pamphlet Spiritism before science. (83)

[3] The Philippine Religion is kept purer in llocos, because there the floods of foreigners should not have mixed; but in their religious terminology it seems that Tagalog times are preserved, indicating their origin. The name of Angngaló is not Ilocano, perhaps it is Itneg. But the Ilocanos sometimes call

the Tagalogs Angalo. And if Angngaló is the same as Angalog, although it seems risky to say so, then it would be the Tagalog par excellence, the Father of all Filipinos. Remember that the Castilianized name of Ilocano or Hoco also comes from ilog, according to the friar chroniclers, so that Ilocano comes to mean the same as tagalog or taga-log and the one who lives on the banks of a river, and in effect, all the Ilocano towns are based on riverbanks. Litaw's (floating) name is more Tagalog than Ilocano; but at least those from Manila no longer remember him, but Siúkuy, who is the same, but with a different name. According to Voltaire, the ancient peoples did not believe in the creation of the first matter. In Sanskrit there is no word that means creation or appearance. Does such an idea appear in the Rig-Veda, in the Zend-Avesta or in Homer," says Lubbock, adding: "For races a little more advanced than the Indigenous tribes, creation is not such? but is only the raising of the earth, already existing at the bottom of the earth. According to the Polynesians of New Zealand, heaven and earth existed from the beginning; but the last one was covered with water until he pulled it out with a Maui or Tangaloa hook, a name that is similar to Angngaló. A perishable thing is told by the indigenous people of Tonga, Samoa and Hervey. The last they point to a two-foot hole in a rock, where said hook was stuck, and this recalls the hole of Aran.

[4] We agree with Lubbock that among the Indigenous person races there are no myths of significance, because they do not know how to form them; but the ancient Filipinos (and the contemporary Ilocos who preserve this mythology), were civilized, and they well knew and know that it is a fable; but it would not be a fable without hidden meaning when it is kept with the affection with which a jewel inherited from parents is preserved. In Madagascar there is no fable about gods and goddesses, to believe Sibree (Madagascar and its People)'. And so it will be among Indigenous person peoples, whose intelligence is not yet cultivated to invent these fictions; but from the

moment in that they already know how to invent fabulous stories of gods, it seems logical to assume that they carry an object when creating them and under those literary forms they will hide an idea or teaching. Let us not forget that all the ancient religions of peoples who already they knew how to speculate, they liked to surround themselves with mysteries, believing that secrecy made their teachings more venerable, august and effective; at the same time that they could thus refine the crude ancient anthropomorphism, giving to the very human stories of their gods abstract meanings. their gods abstract meanings. The Filipinos must have had their myths and mysteries, like even now the holy men who from time to time appear carry their little books full of cabalistic words and signs, which they explain to their own.

[5] The Leni-Lenape, according to Mul'er, say that initially Mánitu swam in the waters (as the Spirit of God of Genesis I, 2) and from a grain of sand - made the earth; and from a tree he formed a man and a woman. The mingos and the attawas believe that it was a rat who made the earth out of a grain of sand. In Lewin's Hill Tracts of Chittagong, we find a creator potter like the one in Genesis. According to him, the Chittagong kumis, God made the world, the trees, the reptiles and lately a man and a woman out of clay; but every night, when the work was finished, 'a snake devoured the clay figures, while the god slept, until he managed to create a dog that scared away the snake. Would it not be possible that chapter III of Genesis has come from the perfection of this crude cosmogony? The admirable thing is that the Chipewyans, according to Dunn, in his Oregon, thought like modern geologists that in the beginning the world was a globe of water, from which the Great Spirit caused the earth to come out.Blumentritt writes to me that traces of gods, demons and giants are found throughout the world: in the vicinity of Leitmeritz (Austria), where he resides, there are in a certain stone some like handprints which the vulgar attribute to him; devil, which is why they are called Teufelspakt (from teufel-

devil, and Platze-big hand of a giant or paw of a lion or tiger).

[6] But not as Colin et al. If the Brahmans are the ones who brought us this legend, then you will find its origin in a legend of theirs, according to which the egg of the world floated on the sea of milk, and after a year, at the divine voice vatchl, it bursts into two halves: the sky and the earth, in the middle the atmosphere, and Brahma was seen in the figure of a child like a lord son (Pati-anak.) rocking on the waves leaning on a lotus flower (baeno in tagalog, according to the great Filipino botanist Dr. León M.a Guerrero). He suddenly became a giant and exclaimed: Who will preserve what I have created? From his own mouth came a bluish spirit that answered: Me. And this one as Angngaló ordered what was created. Blumentritt writes to me: 'The Malays also say they came out of a reed. Those of the islands of Mentawai (W. of Sumatra), those of the SE part, of Borneo (Pasir), those of Holontalo and the alfuros of Minahassa (north Sulawesi), those of Kaborang Island or Abotean [Talaur group] Between Sulawesi and the Philippines they say that the first man was Hoera Boelauro (Hura Bulao). He cut down a vine or rattan on the mountain, and on this vine, he found a man and a woman from whom the said islanders believe they are descended. According to the council, the kings of the alfuros of the island of Ceram bring their origin from the Waringí trees (a species of baliti and others from a coconut tree. Some tribes of Armboyna believe they descend from pieces of cane, others from alligators and crocodiles or eels. They will be like the Igorot's of Lepanto who venerate eels)

[7] (1)The Bachafine Kaffirs believe that things made themselves, the trees and herbs growing by their will (Burchel).(2) I will be very grateful if those who have more news about Anngngaló, and about the King of Creation send them to the Renaissance for its publication; and other data that you think are interesting to complete or rectify my humble opinions and reports.(3) In Benguet, Dúgay is the patron saint of the rice harvest, and

before harvesting it, they dedicate offerings to her by way of the mambúnong.

[8] But yes, among the Tagalog, the King of Creation.

[9] Spiritism is Philosophy, by González Soriano; Book of the Spirits, by Allan Kardec. Etc. Also the mountain people of India, the Chinese and even the civilized Europeans in past times offered meals to their dead, and even now I saw the gypsies of Spain put plates on their graves.

[10] In the Bible nothing is said about the souls of fetuses and unbaptized children, nor about their limbo, which is a pure invention of Romanists, God being incapable of punishing innocent creatures. But it seems indubitable that the idea of the cherubs, which they paint as incomplete children, must have been born from the belief that the souls of fetuses and children become little angels, as we see in the old paintings of the Romanists.

[11] And they did well not to attribute their own bad thoughts, passions and vices to the imaginary demon. There are no such demons, but imperfections or rudeness of matter, which we must polish And there are many natural things that we call sins, but we do not say them as the philosopher, according to whom, capital sins are congenital stimuli for progress; but there is no doubt that everything natural that is not really adulterated by evil cannot be sin, but rather an instinct established by God himself. Man, like every work of God, is endowed with perfectionability; The Creator put that perfectibility in his hands and free will. The fact that he is not yet perfect does not mean that he is not endowed with all the dispositions to reach it. Everything consists in perfecting ourselves according to the natural development of our constant perfectibility, correcting the indignities of matter, its bad inclinations or atavisms; in dignifying ourselves so that we are worthy of our heavenly Father, the prototype of perfection, and thus deserve his mercies

and favors.

[12] The Saxons also speak of a "moon man" they call Mane or Maní, probably the Meni, of Isaiah LXV, n; deus lunus,Printed the previous sheet, the Municipal President of Baguio (Igorot], informs me that the two halves that became children of Lumáwig (see page), were also thunder: the largest is the one that sounds very loud, and the smallest, called Upon is that weak or distant thunder.

[13] Gisbert only says that among the Bagobos, the first name of God is Tiguiama, also Manama and Todlay; and that Todlibon is a pure, holy woman, venerated, especially by women, without having seen or known her; Todlay's wife, although always a virgin. It seems that it means flaming: darang, in Ilocano it is flame. They call the volcano sandaoa or llbóangan. The idea of hell must have been born from the sight of the volcanoes.

[14] (1) The Bible also distinguished spirit from soul, Isaiah LVII,16: Tesalonicians V, 23; Hebrew IV, 12.

[15] The Dayaks of Borneo, the Negrito-Malays of Luwang, Aru, Kei and Babar, up to the ancient Germans, believe that the soul separates from the body during sleep, and the Amazulus affirm that the souls of their parents still live while they appear to them in dreams. The Egyptians believed that reason or intelligence, Khu, was their igneous soul and that it flew into the ether when the body died; while the other soul, Ba, was subjected to the judgment of Osiris, In Ilocano, the shadow is called aniníwan, anínaw, the image in the water, anínag the shadow seen through something transparent; aningaas, is made up of ani (soul) and anges or umanges, what transpires (through the pores), all are formed from the root ani, which, like the Latin soul, means soul or shadow. In Malay, the soul is called ani-ani. We have already said that anito means soul of the dead. The other root of soul is the karahuang of the Malays of Borneo, from which the karkarmá or the Ilocano kararuát are formed; kalaluwa and

kakap in tag.; kalag bisbik.; kamatu among the tirurays.

[16] In Bisaya and bíkol, the shadow is called landong, and landong or lagdon called his idols, which corresponds to ladawan, (iloc.) or larawan (tag.). What does image mean? In Micronesia and Tasmania, the word for soul means shadow (tamune or tamre). The American Indians regard the shadow of man as his soul or life. In my Prehistory of the Philippines, I first called attention to the various denominations of the soul among the Ilocanos. It is called Karkarma, the shadow of man when the body is still alive; alalia or araría when he already died, and aniwaás or aningaas is a name common to both states, dead and alive. And there is another word that corresponds to the alma as the Christians conceive it and it is called kararuá It seems to be araría the soul of the wicked, because it hurts and is fearsome, and kararuá corresponds to that of the just, because it is a word that implies veneration; corresponds to the old word Anito: but kararuá, because of the idea it expresses, seems to be foreign, and probably comes from the karahuang of the olo-ngadjus of Borneo. These various words refer to reason, which was formerly believed to be the same shadow or specter, and with the introduction of Buddhism and Christianity, became a soul. The Dayaks of Borneo believe that when man dies, the soul hambaruan It was. The man observed that other beings and objects, even weapons and utensils, have a shadow and he believed that they also have a soul, doubtless for the afterlife. It divides into two: the lian (alalia) goes to Paradise; the karahuang (which corresponds to the kararua or kalolua of the Filipinos) is suffocated in the body until the tiwah (tibau of the Tagalog's). When the tiwah is celebrated, they invoke the good spirits sangutang, corresponding to the sangunian or guardians or defenders of the ta-galogs) so that they awaken the karahuang and go to join the It'au; It is like the kar-karmá of the Ilocanos, which can be misplaced or lost through carelessness. The Javanese, Buquineses, Malcasars and Malays themselves believe in two souls, or two denominations of souls, which the Malays

themselves call Sumangat and the Javanese Semangot. The Sundanese mention three souls: lelembutan or atji (life, as 103 Hebrews); juni or yuni (will, sympathy, prestige); to the sukma, the soul that thinks. The Dayaks and the Negrito-Malays of Celebes believe that the spirit of each disease enters the body of the sick person and occupies the place of the soul (kambaruan) and invokes the spirits good for expelling the spirit of disease. The peasants of the Philippines believe that the soul of a deceased has entered certain patients, and they expel him by whipping him with thorny branches. The Fijians affirm that a man has two almaí, a black one who is his shadow, he goes to hell. The other is his image reflected in the water or in a mirror and this remains near the place where the body dies. (i) As the Dayaks, the Fijians and surely the other Malays believe. Until that the spiritualists imitated. In a session at the Universal Love Center in Barcelona, I heard a medium say that an image of Christ placed in the fire is destroyed or disintegrates, because it loses its "spirit." Yes, wood has a spirit, he repeated, or its affinity, which meant cohesion, which the chemists called the law of affinity, or of attraction, according to Flanmarian.

[17]   (In Java, Sumatra, Buru and Celebes suppose that in certain alligators and crocodiles there are human souls. These alligators and crocodiles do no harm but defend men against true alligators. The Bataks consider them sacred, inviolable. They call óuWaj'at in the Philippines buwaya Those of the islands of Timor, Baba, Wetter, Ara and Amboina claim descent from caimans. When a new king ascends the throne, they throw a young girl at him who, they believe, marries her. They offer them food and make idols of them. In Hawaii it is assumed that the soul of a man devoured by a shark, reincarnates in it. Even Fray G, from San Agustin , believed that the alligators and crocodiles of the Panay river that devoured a person almost daily, were witches and sorcerers, because, he says, "the hooks that armed them were found hanging from the thinnest of the reeds and trees and sometimes the clothes of those who had

caught without breaking, something that nobody could do but the devil." And he adds: Many things of these and I heard it said in six years that I was in that province, very difficult to believe.

[18] The Indigenous tribes usually identify the victim with the Anito to whom they sacrifice it, considering them equally sacred, just as the Romanists confuse the host with God.

[19] According to another author, the Aino's worship the sun, the wind, the sea and the bear, calling them Kamui (God). They offer 6 fixed small pieces of wood in the name of their gods, as the Catholics offer candles to their saints. The bear, despite being venerated, they eat, praying before doing so. They keep as amulets bird feathers, snake skin and skulls of animals. They thought that dogs spoke at first. A married couple had a dog that spoke. The man went to a forest with that dog, and later he returned to the woman to tell her that his master had been killed by a bear and that before he died, he was annoyed that he should marry the widow. She, scandalized by the trickery, threw into his mouth a handful of earth, and since then the dog has lost his speech.

[20] Shintoism: It is the ancient religion of our neighbors the Japanese, the one that they professed before embracing Buddhism, which in the sixth century of Christ penetrated from China and Korea. It is called Kami no michi (Way of the Gods) and in Sino-Japanese, Sinto. It consists of the cult of the souls of the dead, of the forces of nature and of the Guardian's that live in the air. Apparently, it is similar to our Aniteria. They venerate the spirits of the heroes and benefactors of the town, and they invoke them in their needs and tribulations to protect them. The two male and female principles called Isa-nagi and Isa-nami who come to be cu eros men, begot the sun goddess, Ise, and she ruled Japan. Their descendants, when they died, were deified representing the powers of nature, from them the Mikado's (emperors) descend in a straight line, which are considered as gods even when they are alive. the tradition comes

from the book Chu-king of the Chinese · It preaches respect for the gods, love for the country, admission to the Mikado and its representatives, and obedience to its mandates, to the dictates of one's own conc science and the laws of social morality. In 1868 Shintoism was declared the State religion. Despite this, it is very decayed, and Buddhism prevails, but mixed with Shintoism and modified by the Japanese bonzangs.

[21] The Hebrew prophets compared them to the morning star Isaiah XIV, 12.

[22] Those that in Spain are called tollos are bizcochería, which in the Philippines love soups what we call broas is bizcocho in Spain. Filipino hard biscuits do not exist in Spain, unless they are toasted slices of bread, but not sweet.

[23] Report of the Committee of the Legislative Council or Aborigines, Victoria 1859. (a) Nachrichten von der Amer. Halh California 1773. (3) Gibbs and Schoolcraft, Indian Tribes Burchl, Traveling Dr. Vanderkemp, Moffat and Dr. Gardner, World Religions.

[24] Also, a doctor director of a large hospital in Germany, who had been educated Christian, said to Haeckel: "If it is true that an intelligent God rules in command, he cannot be a God of love, but an omnipotent demon who amuses himself in an eternal game destroying what he built yesterday

[25] Before reaching the printing of this page, I arrived at Norzagaray (Bulacan) and passing the neighborhood of Matiktik, I found in the middle of the river on a protruding rock the supposed imprint of San Cristobal. In fact, it is two-thirds of a yard long and there are six or seven fingerprints (it is not clear). The resemblance is casual and not great. I went to see it in case it was a vestige of the prehistoric "almost grandiose civilization" that Reclus claims to have found in Oceania (Easter Island, and perhaps the Marianas). It didn't seem like such a prehistoric vestige to me; but neither is it ludicrous that some

idle stonemason has entertained himself in fixing it. Who knows if the resemblances of statues that I saw inside the caves of Sibul were really evidence of that?

[26] This anthropomorphism became the trinity of the mysterious source of the Universe, whose three manifestations were: Anu, the original chaos; Belo, the energy that transformed chaos, and Ao, the divine wisdom that presided over everything (later the Holy Spirit or Word); just as the ancient Trimurti of India became Brahma the creator, Siva the destroyer, and Vishnu the preserver, that is, God creates, destroys, and rebuilds.

Made in the USA
Middletown, DE
01 October 2023

39905979R00099